America Remembers World War II

AMERICA REMEMBERS

Alfred A. Knopf  *New York*

WORLD WAR II

V IS FOR VICTORY

KATHLEEN KRULL

THIS IS A BORZOI BOOK PUBLISHED BY ALFRED A. KNOPF

Text copyright © 1995 by Kathleen Krull

www.randomhouse.com/kids

Photograph credits appear at the back of the book.
War map © by Rand McNally, R.L. 95-S-45. Used by permission.
KNOPF, BORZOI BOOKS, and the colophon are registered trademarks of Random
House, Inc.

Library of Congress Cataloging-in-Publication Data
Krull, Kathleen.
V is for victory : America remembers World War II / by Kathleen Krull.
p.   cm.
Includes bibliographical references and index.
ISBN 0-375-81600-3 (pbk.) — ISBN 0-679-96198-4 (lib. bdg.)
1. World War, 1939–1945—United States—Juvenile literature.
[1. World War, 1939–1945.] I. Title.
D769.K78   1995
940.53—dc20   94-28309

Book and cover design by Joy Chu
First paperback edition: May 2002
Printed in the United States of America
10 9 8 7 6 5 4 3 2 1

To the youngest Krulls:

ALLISON,

ANDREW,

BRIAN,

CAITLIN,

COLIN,

ELLIOT,

EMILY,

KEVIN,

and

REBECCA

with hopes for no wars
in their future

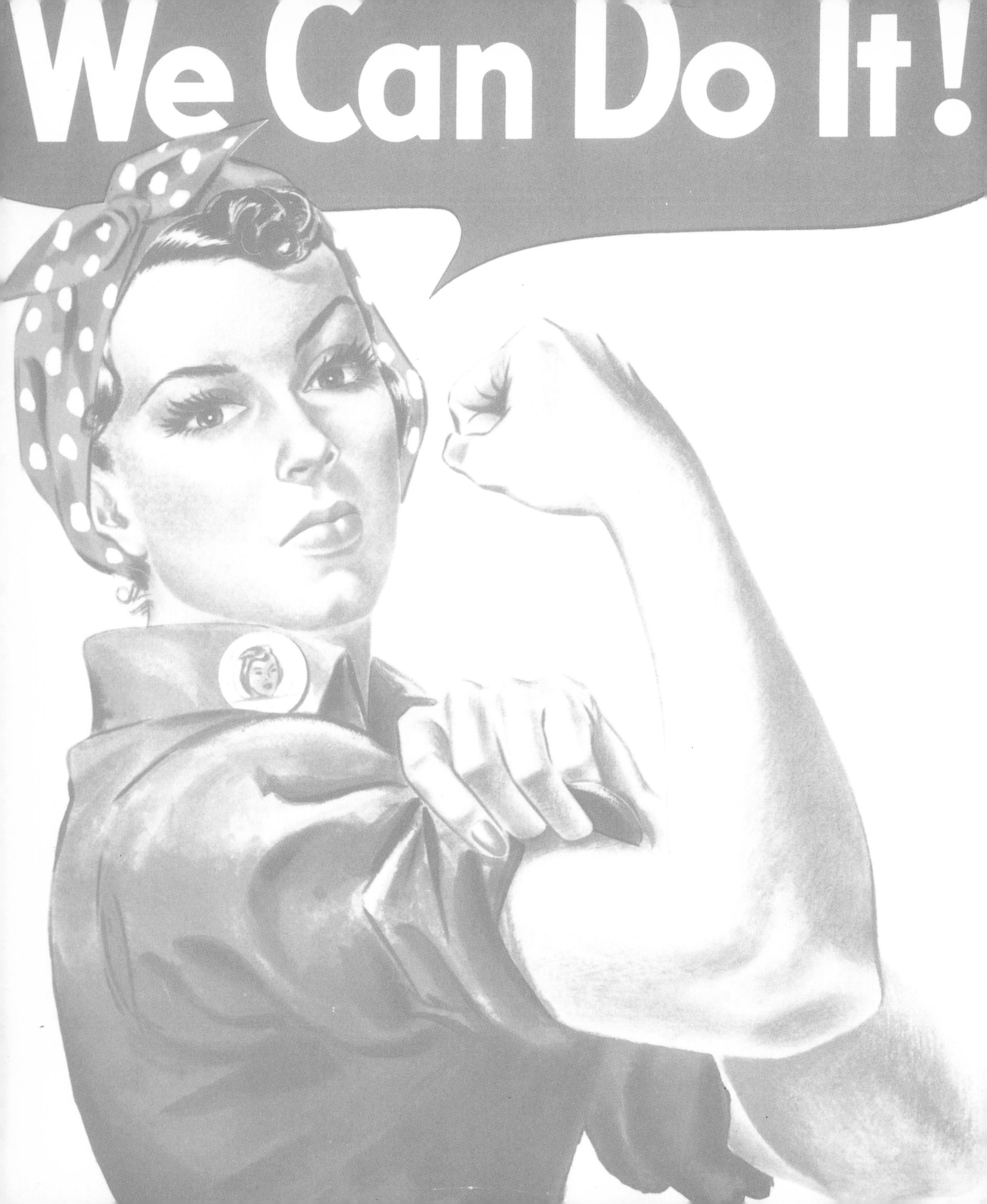
We Can Do It!

ACKNOWLEDGMENTS

I am indebted to Anne Schwartz; Patricia Stone Daniels; Paula Soderlund, photo researcher; and Ada Fitzsimmons of the Paper Pile collectibles store. Thanks also to my father, Ken Krull; Susan Cohen and Barry Berg; Larry Dane Brimner for his generosity and expertise; Jean Ferris and Jessie Schwartz; Sheila Cole; Mary Horschke; Joan Chase Bowden; Peter Neumeyer; Kathryn and David Hewitt; Nancy Holder for German translations; Melanie Brewer for secretarial help; and Paul Brewer.

The day Pearl Harbor was bombed was my father's fourteenth birthday. While he and my grandmother traveled by automobile from Kansas City back to their apartment in Chicago, she became ill with food poisoning and my dad had to take the wheel. He remembers this as the day he first drove a car—and heard the most dramatic news of his life over the radio when he got home. Soon he was making model airplanes in school shop class for use in Army training, and working such long hours after school in a defense plant that he was able to buy his own car at the age of fifteen.

My mother was nine when the war started. To her it seemed a nuisance in her daily life of school plays and games with giggling girlfriends.

I am a postwar baby boomer, born in the year when the death rate from polio—the disease more people dreaded than the possibility of enemy attack—was highest. In high school I remember reading *The Diary of Anne Frank* and being awakened to the horrors of the Holocaust. Now I live in San Diego, one of the American cities that underwent the greatest change during the war.

While I was working on this book, hardly a day went by without newspaper reports of new works of art inspired by the war, or articles directly related to it. Countless aspects still arouse debate—strategy, motives, decisions, the millions of effects and what-ifs. I saw more than ever that understanding *today's* headlines depends on knowing about those of fifty years ago.

Most fascinating to me was the way mention of the war prompted from anyone over age sixty (who would have been six or older in 1941) a torrent of stories—stories that helped me to shape the basic facts of the war into this book.

CONTENTS

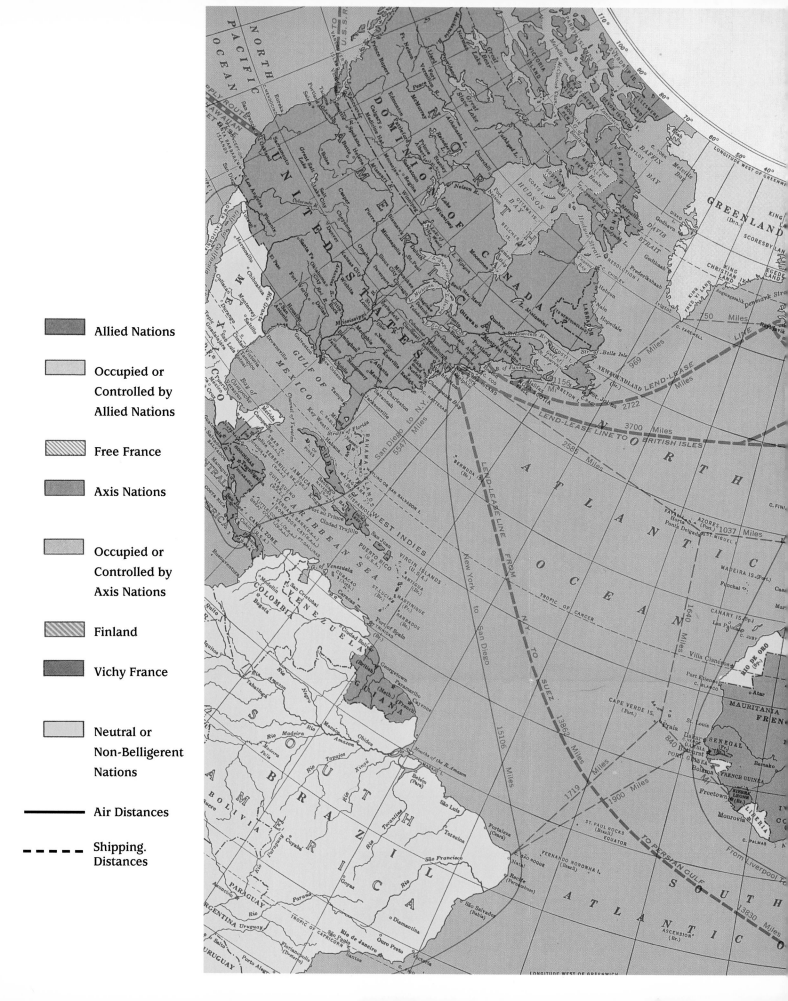

Allied Nations

Occupied or Controlled by Allied Nations

Free France

Axis Nations

Occupied or Controlled by Axis Nations

Finland

Vichy France

Neutral or Non-Belligerent Nations

Air Distances

Shipping. Distances

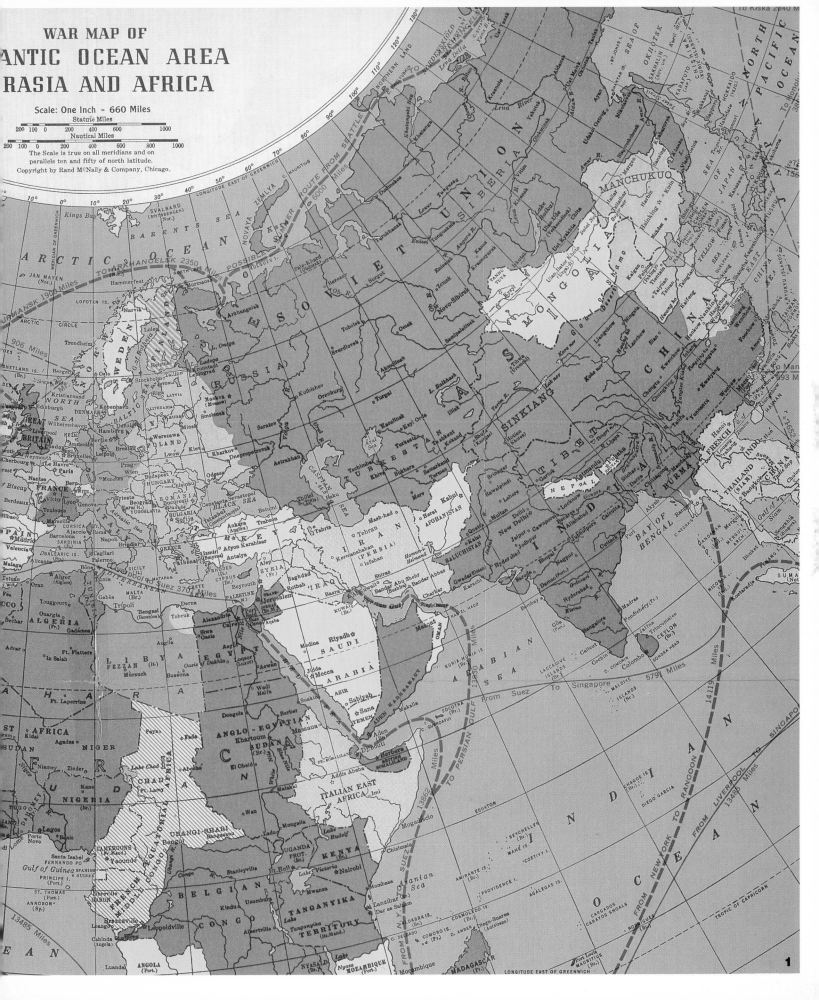

Together for Victory

Although World War II may sound like an event from the misty past, it is closer than you think. Probably no family in the United States today is unaffected by it. The war changed every aspect of people's lives then and continues to influence some area of *your* life now.

Someone in your family may have fought in the military. Perhaps your relatives left farms and moved to cities for jobs in the defense industries. Those who were kids then may have had unusual responsibilities. Your female relatives may have discovered new roles in the workplace and within the family. The range of careers that *you're* contemplating may be a result of opportunities your relatives had in the military or in civilian jobs.

"What you're making may save my Daddy's life"

People in your family may recall aspects of the war years fondly—as the last time this country was truly unified in what felt like a clear struggle between good and evil.

Or they may remember the war as a nightmarish time. Your family may have relatives who were victims of the Nazi mass murder of Jews, or were imprisoned in Japanese internment camps. Your family may have lost their home and been forced to emigrate as refugees.

Although the war involved every major power in the world, it wasn't just

INCREASE PRODUCTION
FOR AXIS DESTRUCTION

about statistics—like all wars, it was about the emotions of individual people, too. This book collects all sorts of experiences, many of them worthy of further study, from the time period when "V" meant "Victory." Other books can tell you about battles, for example. This is a book about people: how the war looked to the families in the United States who were fighting it.

By sharing this book with your own family, you can find out about the different ways the war changed *your* family history. Once you get older relatives started talking about the war, you may not be able to get them to stop.

Among the other lasting effects from the war, it created millions of dramatic stories—of cruelty and hatred, courage and sacrifice, terror and suspense—events so strange as to be unbelievable, but all of them true.

Chapter 1

What would quickly become known as the Second World War was in fact two separate though related wars. One was in the European "theater," where Germany was determined to seize all of Europe and North Africa, while Germany's ally, Italy, tried to dominate the Mediterranean and the Balkans. The second was in the Far Eastern, or Pacific, "theater," where Japan intended to take over Southeast Asia. War erupted when other countries stepped in to stop the aggression of Germany, Italy, and Japan.

The path to such worldwide catastrophe had been a long one.

"The war to end all wars"—that was the name many gave the First World War (1914–1918). After it was over, those who had fought it were exhausted. The winners—the United States, Great Britain, France, and Italy—were determined to avoid future conflicts. With the Treaty of Versailles, they imposed harsh punishment on Germany for its major role in the war—so harsh that Germany was financially bankrupted and morally humiliated.

But World War I was not to be the end of all wars. International tensions quickly began mounting, and by the 1930s the stresses were once again high all around the globe. The cost of fighting had left most countries financially devastated. As in Germany, conditions were ripe for the rise of military dictators who would try to enrich their own countries by invading others. Alarming images began to appear from places where people were suffering.

Italian children, victims of war. Italy came under the dictatorship of Benito Mussolini in 1922. His ambition was to build a great Italian empire. In 1935, he invaded Ethiopia and in 1939, after proclaiming himself emperor, ordered the invasion of Albania.

An injured Chinese baby screams amid the rubble of a wrecked railway terminal, after the Japanese bombing of Shanghai, China, in 1937. This famous photo turned many in the United States against Japan's aggressive policies. Some historians consider 1931—when Japan invaded and seized Manchuria, part of China—the real start of World War II. Japan was undergoing a population explosion. To make up for the scarcity of its own natural resources, the tiny country was attempting to enlarge its borders. Dominated by military leaders, eventually led by General Hideki Tojo, Japan launched a full-scale invasion of China in 1937. During a decade of Japanese aggression against China, over 10 million Chinese people died in what has been called the "forgotten Holocaust."

A ten-year-old girl in Poland grieves for her sister, killed by German machine-gun fire. Some of the most disturbing images of all began to emerge as a result of the rise of the Nazi Party in Germany. Its leader was Adolf Hitler, who ascended to dictatorship in 1933 by vowing to restore Germany's earlier strength. Germany began its conquest of Europe when it took over Austria and Czechoslovakia in 1938. The next year, it invaded Poland.

Hitler had long courted Japan and Italy as valuable partners. By 1940, Germany, Italy, and Japan had aligned themselves under the Tripartite Pact. Known as the Axis powers, they planned to establish a "new order" throughout the world, with Europe to be dominated by Germany and Italy, and Asia to be dominated by Japan.

A British soldier kisses his son good-bye at the train station. France and Great Britain, known as the Allied powers, responded to Germany's invasion of Poland by immediately declaring war on Germany. But the Allies lost battle after battle as Hitler went on to conquer most of Europe. To the rest of the world's shock, even the strong country of France was forced into submission. Then, in 1940, Germany attacked Great Britain, the only European country that hadn't yet surrendered. The city of London was besieged by German bombs. Millions of children were evacuated to live with families in the countryside, where it was considered safe. Those left behind slept in the underground subways, doused the fires from constant explosions, fought back, and refused to surrender.

Parents in the Soviet Union find the body of their son, killed in a Nazi attack. In 1941, Germany invaded the Soviet Union, forcing that huge country and its dictator, Josef Stalin, into the war. Though the Allied powers opposed communism (the Soviet system of government, in which all property was held in common), they became uneasy allies with the Soviet Union. All were united in trying to defeat Germany. For his part, Stalin joined with the Allies only so *he* could take over Europe after Germany was defeated.

The United States was vitally concerned about German aggression. Its worry increased after one of its own ships, the USS *Reuben James*, was attacked by a German U-boat off Iceland and sunk on October 31, 1941, killing 115 men. Hitler by now was at the peak of his power, in control of nearly every European country except Great Britain.

By the fall of 1941, relations between the United States and Japan had reached an impasse. Japan had moved further into China and then into French-occupied Indochina. The United States retaliated by halting trade with Japan—a devastating economic blow. When the United States called for Japan to withdraw, Japanese leaders regarded this as an insult.

No matter how strained the relationships between countries became, the majority of Americans believed we should take care of our own problems first. The stock market had crashed in 1929, creating the Great Depression—a time of widespread poverty and panic. While the Axis powers were gaining control, almost one in five Americans was still out of work. American President Franklin D. Roosevelt and his supporters believed that the United States could help the Allies without getting involved directly. Roosevelt thwarted aggression

indirectly, by sending aid to Britain to fight Germany, and by ordering the American Pacific fleet to a location closer to Japan—Pearl Harbor in Hawaii. A powerful isolationist movement pressured Roosevelt to keep the United States out of the war. Letters urging a neutral position came into the Senate mailroom at a rate of 200,000 a day. Conflicting opinion polls showed that Americans felt war was inevitable, but not that it was desirable.

Still, most agreed that if Britain fell to the Nazis, the United States would have no security and would have to fight. And one prewar poll showed 70 percent of Americans in favor of risking war to stop Japan. Nevertheless, to win a third term as president in 1940, Roosevelt promised American voters, "Your boys are not going to be sent into any foreign wars."

The United States was like a "sleeping giant"—a powerful force not yet aware of what was about to happen.

◀ A Depression-era family from Hanford, California.

AND THE FIRST DAYS OF AMERICAN INVOLVEMENT

Then came the sunny Sunday morning of December 7, 1941. With no warning, planes bearing the Japanese insignia of the rising sun attacked one of the least-expected places: Pearl Harbor, the United States naval base on the Hawaiian island of Oahu.

At 7:55 A.M., American servicemen at Pearl Harbor were eating breakfast or still sleeping. As the first bombs exploded, they assumed that the noise was some type of mistake—an American plane misfiring, or perhaps a practice drill. Then, from the battleship *Oklahoma*'s loudspeakers, came the message: "Real planes, real bombs; this is no drill!"

A Japanese aerial photograph shows the first few minutes of the assault on Pearl Harbor. Fires rage in the background, destroying American planes that could have fought back. A trail of torpedoes streaks toward the battleship *West Virginia*, already hit and leaking oil. The other ships, moored along Battleship Row, have already been or are just about to be bombed.

American servicemen rushed heroically to defend the base, but conditions were against them. Guns sat unmanned and without ammunition. Many sailors, used to taking weekends off, were absent. The American warships and fighter planes had been placed in a peacetime condition of readiness—not geared for attack. Even worse, the planes were parked on the ground together; they were easy targets.

Hundreds are dying as this photograph is being taken. As the bombs hit, concrete, glass, and metal fly everywhere. On the left, the call of "Abandon ship!" has been made, and the crew of the *California* is evacuating over the side. In the background, black smoke billows out of the *Oklahoma*, which has already capsized, drowning all 415 aboard. Spilled oil engulfs those trying to make it to shore.

In the center is the burning *Arizona*, ripped apart by an explosion, about to capsize. Fewer than 200 of the 1,400 men aboard will survive. The previous evening, the *Arizona*'s band had won second place in a contest. The band members were rewarded by being allowed to sleep in late on Sunday morning. As a result, the entire band died when their ship went down. They were all between eighteen and twenty years old.

The Japanese assault took less than two hours and left 2,403 Americans dead. For days afterward, the dead were buried and a bouquet of flowers was placed on each grave. The wounded—1,178 people—were treated at the Army Hospital, where volunteers waited up to seven hours to donate blood; the staff ran out of containers and began filling sterilized Coke bottles.

The day was a total victory for the Japanese, who hit almost every target they had intended to and lost only 64 men. It was the worst military defeat in American history—one of the most devastating strikes in the history of warfare. Only one or two American planes succeeded in getting airborne, whereas the Japanese lost only 29 of their 360 planes.

The effect of the sneak attack was to wipe out America's air and sea power in the Pacific. It left Japan free to take control of that part of the world. Within twenty-four hours after Pearl Harbor, Japan attacked Malaya, Hong Kong, Guam, the Philippines, Wake Island, and Midway Island.

A Redding, California, newsboy selling newspapers on December 7, 1941. Newspapers were snapped up once the first reports of the attack came over the radio. Those who were alive that day can recall exactly what they were doing when they heard the news—coming home from church or a movie matinee, getting ready for Sunday dinner, listening to the Sunday afternoon concert of the New York Philharmonic or to the big football game between the Washington Redskins and the Philadelphia Eagles. Not everyone was quite clear on Pearl Harbor's significance, but even children could tell from their parents' reactions that this was a moment of danger and outrage. For some, it was the first time they had seen a parent cry.

The following day, President Roosevelt asked Congress to declare war on Japan: "Yesterday, December 7, 1941—a date which will live in infamy—the United States of America was suddenly and deliberately attacked...." His radio address grabbed the largest audience in history—90 million people, or virtually every adult in the country.

Within the hour, Congress voted to declare war. The vote was unanimous, except for the "no" vote from pacifist Jeannette Rankin, representative from Montana (who had also voted no on World War I).

In short order, Japan's partners Germany and Italy declared war on the United States, and Congress declared war on them.

The United States was now fully engaged in World War II.

This newspaper headline, written four days after Pearl Harbor, describes the blackout of the entire Los Angeles–San Diego region. In the early days of the war, many Americans panicked. Panic was especially intense on the West Coast—closest to Japan—but common in other cities as well. Rumors ran wild. Were enemy warplanes flying over California cities every night? Was the United States really full of enemy dogs, barking in a code only the Japanese could understand?

One reason why the Japanese attack had caught the United States so off guard was ignorance. The average American knew little about Asians, and many had deep-rooted racist attitudes. Japanese were portrayed in print as "Japs," and stereotyped as mere makers of inexpensive toys.

Emergency window coverings prevent light from showing through windows and making a house a target for bombers.

Two illustrations of what not to do during an air-raid drill: Do *not* look out the window (this boy may not mean to, but is flashing a signal to enemy planes), and do *not* panic (this girl is doing just what the enemy wants).

Instead, when the sirens howled, families were supposed to get inside and go quietly to the basement, or the room with the fewest windows, taking along warm clothes, flashlights, a radio, and plenty of things to read and do until the raid was over.

Emergency window coverings prevent light from showing through windows and making a house a target for bombers. In the days following Pearl Harbor, children helped their parents protect homes against possible air raids. No light, not even flashlights or matches, was allowed during an alarm. Eerie air-raid sirens sounded day and night. The alarms always turned out to be false (the result of hysteria, or of primitive radar equipment), or just a drill.

But kids, especially, took them seriously. By this time, many were having nightmares about what would happen next. Everywhere, grown-ups were talking about war, and the news was usually bad. With all the rumors about invasion, the sound of any plane could be scary. Kids ran to and from school, worrying that they would be killed by bombs or gunfire. In some cities, children were fingerprinted or wore I.D. tags, to identify them in case they were wounded. The top-selling book of 1942 was the Red Cross first-aid manual—with eight million copies sold.

But for all of the American worries about enemy attacks, no World War II battles were ever fought on American soil. In fact, there were only six casualties on the home front— five of them children. Japan, increasingly desperate later in the war, sent bombs attached to balloons across the ocean, trying to set devastating forest fires along the West Coast. Most either failed to go off or did so in remote areas. The only balloon bomb known to have harmed anyone fell in Oregon. It killed Elyse Mitchell, a pastor's wife, and five Sunday school children on a fishing outing.

Servicemen in Washington, D.C., board a bus at the Greyhound terminal. Perhaps more upsetting for kids than air-raid sirens was the fact that so many of their fathers were leaving for military service. Pearl Harbor initiated a painful and anxious period—between one and four years—of waiting for fathers, brothers, and uncles to return home. Some very young children got confused, thinking every man in uniform was their father, or that every airplane passing overhead carried their father.

But intense patriotism now united the country. The dominant mood had changed from isolationist to pro-war. Men and women all over the United States did not wait to be drafted, but rushed to sign up. Enthusiastic kids as young as twelve and thirteen tried to join them.

Recruiting poster outside the post office in Benton Harbor, Michigan. For those who delayed in enlisting, reminders like the famous "Uncle Sam Wants You" were persuasive. Eighteen- and nineteen-year-olds were bombarded with messages to join the military.

I WANT YOU
for the U.S. ARMY
ENLIST NOW
U.S. Army Recruiting Office

In Portland, Oregon, a war-bond rally featuring Hollywood actress Lana Turner draws a crowd of 25,000. What struck many people most about the days immediately following Pearl Harbor was the amazing way the country seemed to instantly mobilize. One priority was money with which to buy guns, planes, tanks, and ships. The government raised taxes, but it also went directly to the people. Everyone was urged to buy war bonds, which were like loans to the government: you paid $18.75 for a bond that in ten years could be redeemed for $25. It cost $304 billion for the United States to wage World War II, of which one-sixth was covered by war bonds.

Since movies were the most popular form of entertainment, movie stars were used to attract people to huge war-bond rallies. The gatherings spotlighted the Marx Brothers, Lucille Ball, Fred Astaire, Judy Garland, and others.

Posters everywhere urge people to buy war bonds, while "We Gave" stickers mark patriotic homes that have already contributed. Civilians contributed more to this war than to any in United States history. Buying war bonds encouraged a sense of personal involvement, making other sacrifices easier to bear.

During World War II, differences between most Americans seemed to become less significant—the majority were now pulling together in a spirit of a shared mission. War was disruptive for everyone, but life seemed simple and people stuck together. Unlike many other conflicts in American history, this war seemed to have clear good and evil sides. The United States saw the Axis powers as "evil," and itself as the salvation of the "good" side. In the months following Pearl Harbor, kids grew more reassured that bombs were not likely to fall here. Eventually, most came to feel invincible, as if nothing would ever happen to them because they were American.

In recent years, there has been speculation that President Roosevelt knew in advance about the attack on Pearl Harbor—and did nothing because he also knew that its shock would unite the United States behind him in war as nothing else could. However, this theory has never been proved, and few believe it to be true. Another question is what would have happened if the United States had remained neutral: with the ever more powerful weapons Germany was developing, most historians agree that Europe and Asia would have been taken over by the Axis countries.

But December 7 had jolted the "sleeping giant" awake. The country was galvanized in a way it never had been before or has been since. People were ready to go to war, and they had a motto to spur them on: "Remember Pearl Harbor!"

At school, children keep albums of 10- and 25-cent stamps. As they saved allowances and skipped lunch, kids could accumulate enough stamps to exchange for a war bond. Satisfaction came from being able to calculate exactly what they were buying: kids at a Kansas school figured out that their $331 in stamps paid for one machine gun, one telephone, one tent, five steel helmets, and nine tools. In one year alone, school sales of war bonds bought 2,900 planes and 44,000 jeeps.

Chapter 3

ON THE HOME FRONT

Aside from the American flag, "V Is for Victory" became the most common symbol of commitment to the war effort. The government encouraged families to take the "V Home Pledge," which read in part: "We know this war will be easy to lose and hard to win. We mean to win it. Therefore we solemnly pledge all our energies and all our resources to the fight for freedom."

Whether or not they took the "V Home Pledge," families found their routines altering. Compared to what other countries were suffering, war was more of a nuisance than a hardship on the American home front—you couldn't travel, plan dinner, or dress up without being affected by shortages.

But many who were kids then remember these as the most thrilling years of their lives—memorizing the different types of warplanes, watching war movies where the Allies always won, and singing "The Star-Spangled Banner" before baseball games, a tradition that began during the war. Energy-saving measures that we think of as common today—carpooling, recycling—were new and exciting concepts then.

For young and old, life seemed more worth living; indeed, suicides in the United States declined by one-third between 1940 and 1944. The war seemed to equalize society: everyone had to live with rationing, everyone was eligible for military service. It was a time of generosity, and it was a time of change.

The four McLelland children (above) look over the cabbage in their Victory garden in Escambia County, Florida. Families, no matter where they lived, were urged to start growing their own vegetables in "Victory gardens." The less food people bought from stores, the more would be available for soldiers. Gardens appeared everywhere there was soil—parks, schoolyards, even prison yards. By 1942, 21 million families had planted gardens.

Victory cookbook. War changed the way people ate. New cookbooks told how to "feed your family in wartime" with lots of homegrown vegetables. To save meat, soybeans and peanuts were recommended. One-dish dinners—"for housewives who work"—included frankfurter casserole and meat-and-vegetable pie. "Uncle Sam needs us *strong*," women were told, and it was only patriotic to keep families healthy with low-cost foods. Should any children complain, they would hear this refrain: "Think of the poor starving children in Europe."

VICTORY COOK BOOK

How to
EAT WELL ... LIVE WELL ...
PLAN BALANCED MEALS ...
under
FOOD RATIONING

FREE with purchase of LYSOL

Train tickets feature Victory-garden themes and urge kids to join the American Junior Red Cross. Printed material kept the symbolism of the war in front of people in ways that were upbeat and positive. Soldiers were always good-looking and healthy; home-front civilians were always cheerful.

A magazine cover designed to inspire pride in the United States. What did tomato juice, tea, crackers, keys, beer, and black olives have in common? Only proof that any company could use the war in advertisements to sell any product, no matter how unlikely. A cosmetics ad told women, "Your first duty is your beauty—America's inspiration—morale on the home front is the woman's job." Even an ad for pills relieving menstrual cramps features a member of the United States Cadet Nurse Corps being told, "You should make a good nurse—you're so smart about cramps!"

JULY 3, 1942

THE FAMILY CIRCLE

VOL. 21 NO. 1

UNITED WE STAND

The push for victory is launched even in the country's churches. Church organizations turned out to be vital to the war effort. Church attendance soared during the war, as did sales of the Bible.

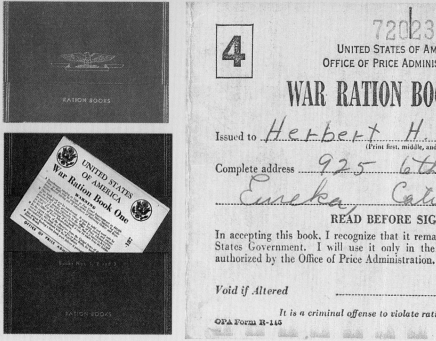

4

720237 M 75¢

UNITED STATES OF AMERICA
OFFICE OF PRICE ADMINISTRATION

OFFICE OF PRICE
ADMINISTRATION
OPA

WAR RATION BOOK FOUR

Issued to _Herbert H. Stuart_
(Print first, middle, and last names)

Complete address _925 6th St.,_

Eureka, Calif

READ BEFORE SIGNING

In accepting this book, I recognize that it remains the property of the United States Government. I will use it only in the manner and for the purpose authorized by the Office of Price Administration.

Void if Altered

....
(Signature)

It is a criminal offense to violate rationing regulation

OPA Form R-145

LET'S SHARE
OUR CARS
AND SPARE
OUR TIRES

230 861

Ration books that families used to buy basics. Even a trip to the store was no longer a simple affair. With any item that could be of use reserved for the military, civilians were allowed only limited amounts. The government distributed books of stamps good for things like butter, meat, cooking fat, canned goods, and shoes. Once you used up your stamps, you weren't supposed to buy any more of that item. Some people cheated—by hoarding items, using other people's stamps, or buying goods illegally on the "black market." But most took pride in "making do" and got used to hearing "Don't you know there's a war on?" from those who saw waste.

As the war continued, shortages became more and more of a headache. Fuel oil for heating homes, batteries, laundry soap, facial tissues, pencils with erasers, safety pins, cotton diapers—all got harder for civilians to obtain. Many meats became unavailable, except for horse meat, which was unrationed. Paper rationing limited book production, and elastic shortages meant that underwear was now fastened with a bow. With nylon going to make parachutes, nylon stockings disappeared; women drew lines on the back of their legs to simulate stocking seams. To save cloth, hems were shorter and cuffs disappeared.

A long line of people waiting for sugar reflects how much people crave it. Sugar and coffee were the first two things to be rationed. Sugar cane could be converted into gunpowder, torpedo fuel, dynamite, and other wartime chemicals. For kids, candy was now a luxury, and chewing gum was the most missed item of all.

Office workers in Highland Park, Illinois, share a ride, while their sign urges, "How about it, neighbor?" As manufacturing shifted into a military mode, civilian needs ran a distant second place—which meant no new refrigerators, stoves, radios, vacuum cleaners, and other appliances on the home front. The last civilian car made during the war was a gray Pontiac in 1942—after that, factories turned out trucks, tanks, and jeeps. Tires and gasoline were strictly rationed, and driving a car became unpatriotic unless it was a necessity. The speed limit across the country was thirty-five miles per hour, to conserve gas. Carpooling was one solution. Adults also rode bicycles to work when possible—creating a shortage of bikes for kids.

Wisconsin's Dane County Boy Scouts display aluminum that residents have donated to the government. Scouting groups were especially active in projects geared to the war. Recycling became a patriotic duty, with any form of scrap metal collected and reused for military needs. An old lawn mower could be turned into three six-inch shells, or a steam iron into thirty hand grenades. The biggest scrap drive was in Nebraska, which in 1942 collected the equivalent of 103 pounds for every Nebraskan.

Meanwhile, in Chicago, Wednesday was "Paper Day." Within a five-month period, kids collected 18,000 tons of newspapers for recycling.

A girl donates her doll for rubber scrap. With most rubber coming from areas now under Japanese rule, it was the material most needed by the American military and in shortest supply on the home front. Scrap could be melted down and reused to make planes and tanks—each tank required one ton of rubber. No one wanted to be accused of wasting rubber. Even in wartime movies, the sound of screeching tires was toned down to reduce the appearance of extravagance. Some younger children had their proudest moments in giving up favorite toys for the war.

WHAT CAN I DO

THE CITIZEN'S HANDBOOK FOR WAR

ISSUED BY:
UNITED STATES OFFICE OF CIVILIAN DEFENSE

<u>The Citizen's Handbook for War</u>, with a chapter on "What Boys and Girls Could Do." Kids had all kinds of new responsibilities at home, at school, and around town. No person was too small to contribute. If children baby-sat and did housework, parents were freed up for war jobs. Kids over fourteen could work on farms during the summer to increase food production, while those who knew how to type could help their neighborhood Defense Council. They sent letters and presents to patients in war hospitals, trapped rattlesnakes to supply venom to protect troops from snakebites, volunteered pet dogs for service, raised carrier pigeons, and collected milkweed pods for the fluff to fill life jackets.

Such tasks were not a burden for most kids, but rather led to feelings of self-worth and genuine usefulness. By becoming part of a team, and trying to outdo or keep up with adults, they gained a sense of involvement in a cause larger than themselves.

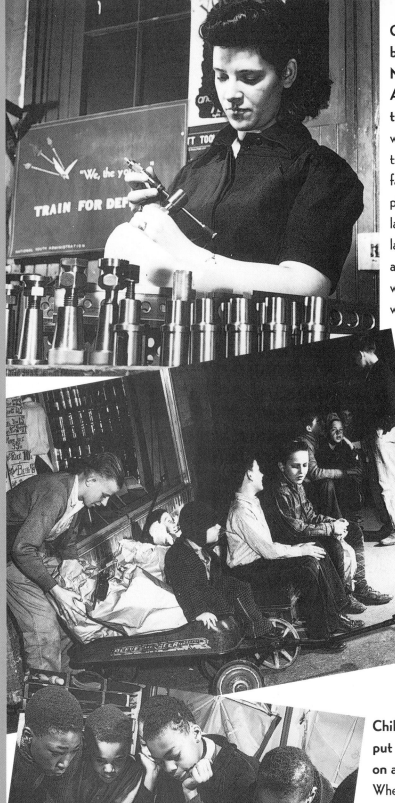

Checking gauges to be shipped from a National Youth Administration shop to a war agency. A whole program put teens to work at factory jobs in defense plants. In many states, laws forbidding child labor were set aside, and by 1943 there were three million working boys and girls.

Enterprising kids in Greenbelt, Maryland, start a wagon service to help carless shoppers get their groceries home.

Children from Chicago put the finishing touches on a model airplane. When the government asked schoolboys to make 500,000 airplane models for use in teaching aircraft recognition to the Army and Navy, high school shop classes were put to work.

breakfast like a bird
and work like a horse!

THIS IS A GOOD BREAKFAST

Grapefruit, orange juice, melon or berries. Coffee.
Oatmeal or other cereal with milk. Eggs now and then.
2 slices whole wheat or enriched bread and butter.

A Walt Disney poster prepared for the Food and Nutrition Committee of the California War Council. All the rationing and sacrifice was never meant to be at the expense of a child's health and well-being. Here kids are told that eating a good breakfast is just as important as their war work.

Booklet published for parents and teachers by the National Education Association. As the number of working teens increased, the number of students in schools decreased—more than a million kids dropped out to earn high wartime wages. Though children were considered vital to the war effort, dropping out of school was not officially encouraged. This wartime publication stresses the importance of school: "The education of America's children cannot be slighted without permanently disastrous results."

Instead, schools were meant to train future war workers, instruct in first aid, help with rationing and war-bond sales, organize air-raid drills, and most of all teach children to be "good strong Americans." By 1944, the curriculum was saturated with patriotism. Music classes taught military marching songs, and reading groups were divided not into redbirds and bluebirds but into corporals and sergeants.

Students at the University of Alabama gather for Red Cross knitting work. Knitting mittens, sweaters, scarves, and socks for soldiers was a favorite wartime activity, a worthy job that was also sociable.

Mother taking charge during an air-raid drill. With many fathers overseas, women were discovering new roles as strong leaders in the home. During the war, almost one in five families was a single-parent one, headed by a woman. Moms were now the ones who changed tires, fixed faucets, and paid the bills. This family is protecting itself under a heavy table, a place recommended to go if bombs were to start falling nearby.

Women received mixed messages about working outside the home. Propaganda urged them to get jobs, yet the housewife was still considered the model woman. In a time of few conveniences (half of American women still did laundry by hand or with hand-cranked machines), housework was a full-time job—fifty hours a week for the average wife and mother.

The symbol worn on the arms of air-raid wardens. More than three million women volunteered for the Red Cross, while 25,000 joined the Women's Ambulance and Defense Corps of America (their slogan was "The Hell We Can't"). Trained as security guards and air-raid wardens, they patrolled neighborhoods, checking homes for ways they might be attracting enemy attention.

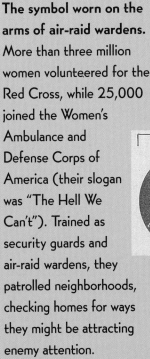

Air Raid Warden

We

Rosie the Riveter shows off her muscles. More women were now working outside the home than ever before. By 1943, they made up one-third of the workforce. They filled jobs left vacant by men in the service, or took new jobs created by wartime. Women worked on the railroads, in steel mills and munitions factories, in meatpacking plants and lumberyards. Most notably, they built B-17 bombers, the famous Flying Fortresses. The percentage of women in the aviation industry went from 1 percent in 1941 to 65 percent in 1943. The workforce at one Minneapolis, Minnesota, company that designed high-altitude pressure suits for pilots was 100 percent women, including the company head; the only male was a department-store dummy.

Rosie was based on a real person, but became a catch phrase for women workers in defense industries. Riveters worked in teams: one woman shot a rivet into metal plates with a gun, while the other flattened it on the opposite side.

For most women, a paycheck was a new concept. The best-paying jobs were in war industries, but here, as in other fields, women were always paid less than men. The minimum rate paid to men was usually higher than the maximum rate paid to women doing the same job.

Welders in a Connecticut factory. By 1945, more than half of all manufacturing in the world was taking place within the United States. Our production surpassed that of all the Allied and Axis powers combined. At their peak, assembly lines could turn out a jeep every two minutes, a Liberty cargo ship every ten hours, a plane every five minutes, a B-24 bomber every sixty-three minutes. Unemployment was all but eliminated. Convicts could get out of jail by volunteering to work in factories; midgets were hired for work in cramped sections of B-24 bombers at Willow Run, Michigan; blind people sorted screws and nuts; and deaf people operated machinery too noisy for other workers.

With safety on the job not monitored as closely as it is today, factory work could be risky. People were not always trained adequately and were under constant pressure to produce. By 1944, people injured on the job outnumbered those injured in battle.

A shipyard worker in Orange, Texas, leaves her daughter at a nursery school at 6 A.M. and arranges to pick her up at 6 P.M. For women who worked forty-eight hours a week with frequent overtime, the need for day care was urgent. Many schools extended their hours, while grandparents and older siblings became increasingly indispensable. Later in the war, the government opened 2,800 child-care centers, but these still served only one out of ten children. A new term that came out of the war was "latchkey children," describing those who carried their own house keys and returned to empty homes after school.

25

An Army sergeant stationed in Fort Knox, Kentucky, marries an Arkansas woman. The year 1941 saw the largest number of American marriages in history, with 1942 breaking that record. Marriage bureaus were so crowded that police were sometimes called to maintain order. With the return of full employment, people felt hopeful financially. But in other respects, the future looked uncertain. People wanted to marry before the war cut off all opportunity. Some women feared that the supply of men would run out; some men hoped that marriage would exempt them from military service. It was a time of impetuousness—people made grand gestures and relationships were intense. By 1943, the supply of wedding rings was dangerously low.

Nine months after the attack on Pearl Harbor, more babies were born than in any month for the previous eighteen years. By 1945, a poll showed that women wanted to have an average of 4.2 children each. The war years were to begin the greatest baby boom in United States history.

Crowds in San Francisco wait in line for housing information. The rising birthrate was just one reason for a severe housing shortage during World War II. Never in American history had so many moved in so many different directions in so short a time. Not counting those in the military, some 30 million people moved for job-related reasons to military bases and industrial boomtowns, mostly in the West. Many moved more than once, uprooting kids from their schools and friends. Some families already on the move, such as Mexican-American migrant farm workers, found jobs in cities and needed housing.

In the boomtowns, people lined up, hoping that a vacant house, a room, or even a bed would be available before the end of the day. Housing was particularly a problem for southern blacks and others who faced prejudice. Some families had to double up, while the "Share Your Home" campaign made it patriotic to take in lodgers.

A storefront window in Galva, Illinois, pays tribute to every single resident serving in the military. Those in the various branches of the military were never far from the minds of those on the home front.

Anyone in the service was considered a hero, and almost one of every five families contributed one or more of its members to it. Home-front towns honored them with displays like this one—which may hail "our boys," but portrays "our girls" as well.

This postcard from a Wisconsin soldier stationed in England reflects a common situation. "Ann wrote that you'd sold the farm," the soldier writes wistfully to his parents, "so I hope you're settled in town now." The direction for most Americans was off the farm and toward the cities.

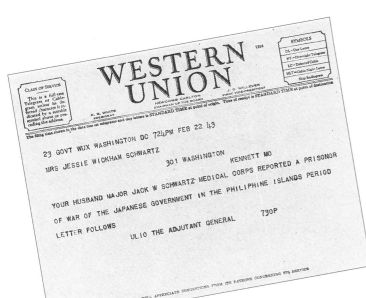

A telegram tells of a husband and father of two, now held as a Japanese prisoner of war. More dreaded than any other sight was a Western Union deliveryman or a military officer at a family's front door. Telegrams from the War Department in Washington were almost never good news, but rather a message that a family's loved one was dead, wounded, or missing in action.

About 183,000 children on the home front lost their fathers. Grief affected many more—everyone had friends who lost someone.

A Marine's family tunes in to the radio in San Diego, California. Families anxiously followed the news of the war on the radio, now the gathering place in most homes. Kids had to keep quiet, and sometimes the room was allowed to go dark, except for the radio's glow. Seventy-five percent of Americans used radio as their major source of war news, which so dominated airtime that some kids thought radio had been invented to convey it. Families got images of war from *Life* magazine photos, black-and-white movie newsreels called "The Eyes and Ears of the World," and their imaginations. Many families also kept maps on display, using pins to mark battles overseas. Sales of maps increased

Superman spends the war years fighting our enemies. So did Batman, and Captain America in his red, white, and blue tights. Birthday parties had war themes, as did jump-rope rhymes and comic books, which were read faithfully by 90 percent of kids between six and eleven years old. Trying to emulate their heroes overseas, kids staged mock battles and often dressed in military outfits such as sailor suits. For boys in particular, it was assumed that if the war lasted long enough, they would eventually be fighting it themselves.

600 percent during the war years. But radio gave a sense of immediacy that nothing else did, especially when news was delivered in the deep voice of famed broadcaster Edward R. Murrow. (Television had been invented, but was being used experimentally for military training only.)

Kids listened to the radio an average of fourteen hours a week. Even adventure serials like "Jack Armstrong, the All-American Boy" became patriotic and war-oriented. "Dick Tracy" listeners took a five-point pledge "to save water, gas, and electricity; to save fuel oil and coal; to save my clothes; to save Mom's furniture; to save my playthings."

A GI's photo scrapbook of his days at Camp Hulen, Texas. He writes that he "fell in plenty on these," to describe a particularly grueling workout. Basic training, or boot camp, entailed rigorous discipline intended to mold men into fighting machines that worked together as a team.

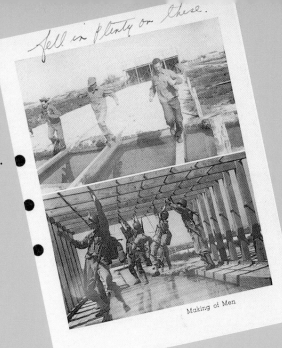

fell in plenty on these.

Making of Men

WAVES

Monday a.m.

Dear Mums, Daddy & Sweens —

Just this minute got off the phone and even though I am still in tears I feel so darn much better talking to you. I have been homesick — I guess because I am separated from all my pals. I got so furious while talking to you because some girl (the Mate of the Deck) popped in and told me to get out! I had been trying to get the call to you since eight o'clock yesterday and tried again right after morning mess. I was in the booth when they called 'Study Hour' and the call was going thru and I wouldn't have left for anything. Where I got out she really gave me heck and when someone gives you heck in the Navy you don't talk back. So what could I do? They are very strict around here and especially during study hour there is absolutely

Letter from a homesick private (below) stationed at Fort Bliss, Texas. "Don't ever try to come in the army," he writes to his civilian friend. "It's plain hell." He adds a plaintive request: "But for gosh sakes why can't you write just once and give me the dirt of the town? Honest, I would like to hear from you."

A twenty-two-year-old WAVE sends a tear-stained letter to her family in Oakland, California. "Just this minute got off the phone," she writes, "and even though I am still in tears I feel so darn much better talking to you. I have been homesick—I guess because I am separated from all my pals."

In a later letter, she pleads, "Mums, will you please buy me some pajamas? I looked all over this stupid, dirty, stinking town for some tailored pj's and couldn't find a thing...you know the kind I like."

Hi Jim

Well Jim I hope the Christmas is a good one. Don't ever try to come in the army its plain hell you can do better on the world on the outside. I really mean that do anything you can to at out. Thanks for the money out it shure helped me out of a jam I'll be able to say it back in a few months. But for gosh sake why can't you write just once and give me the dirt of the town honest I would like to hear now. Well Jim the best

Army C rations—three meals a day. The typical main courses were meat and beans, or meat and vegetable hash. The food was precooked and could be heated up. On the front, where fires would attract enemy attack, it was usually eaten cold. An accessory pack contained luxuries like cigarettes, toilet paper, razor blades, shaving soap, and—through special arrangements—Coke and Wrigley's gum. One food GIs got thoroughly sick of was Spam, or spiced ham, a canned meat developed just before the war.

Soldiers reminisced constantly about food from home. Little things meant a lot. Cokes, for example, became so cherished overseas as to seem a symbol of all the United States was fighting for.

U.S. ARMY FIELD RATION C BREAKFAST UNIT

U.S. ARMY FIELD RATION C DINNER UNIT

U.S. ARMY FIELD RATION C SUPPER UNIT

Army soldiers in bunk beds aboard a ship leaving San Francisco. Military sleeping quarters were cramped, neat, and impersonal. Sleep was treasured, especially when you were surrounded by snorers, or when it was cut short by predawn blasts of bugles.

33

Members of the "First All-Negro Division" of the 93rd Infantry stand poised for action in their trench. Life in the trenches was dirty and dangerous. Hazards included bullets, grenades, and land mines—the buried bombs that blow up when stepped on.

After the war, veterans claimed that unless you were there you really couldn't understand the experience of combat; it combined much waiting and boredom with horrors hard to put into words. Combat soldiers disagree about which American troops faced the worst conditions. One experienced general insisted that the harshest battlefields were the Italian mountains in winter. Many would claim New Guinea was worse, for its "jungle rot" (ulcers all over), clouds of biting insects, leeches, malaria, and dysentery, which felled five for every one man wounded in combat.

A Marine catches a nap in Iwo Jima while guarded by his war dog, Butch. Those in combat used foxholes, or trenches dug at top speed, for temporary protection. In trench warfare, one group fired at the enemy while another group rushed for the next cover.

Japanese-American soldier with captured Italian prisoners of war. Ironically, the military included many whose ancestors came from countries with which America was at war.

Military service threw all types of people together, forcing them to learn tolerance. Some friendships forged in the service lasted a lifetime.

Although homosexuals served during World War II, there is no way to estimate the number; from 1941 on, homosexuality was listed as a disqualification for service, leading homosexuals to keep their sexual orientation private.

An African-American soldier guards prisoners of war in Germany. Perhaps most ironic of all was the role of black soldiers during the war. This was a time when many signs around the United States still read "Colored" and "White" for building entrances, drinking fountains, bathrooms. Attacks on African-Americans occurred every day, especially in the South, where lynchings continued throughout the war. Meanwhile, more than one million blacks were defending their country.

According to a poll, three out of four blacks believed that white and black soldiers should train together, while nine out of ten whites believed they should not. The two groups were kept segregated throughout the war. The American Red Cross even kept donated blood from blacks separate from that of whites.

Blacks in the military were subject to humiliations and obstructions every day. When trying to get from a military base into town, they had to sit in the back of the bus. German and Italian prisoners of war detained in the United States were given preferential treatment over American blacks. In Kansas, for example, black soldiers were not allowed to enter restaurants where German POWs were having lunch.

Marine Corps reservists stationed in Camp Lejeune, North Carolina—Minnie Spotted Wolf (a Blackfoot Indian), Celia Mix (a Potawatomi), and Viola Eastman (a Chippewa). Some 25,000 American Indians served in the military; in some tribes as many as 70 percent of the men enlisted. Unlike blacks, Indians weren't segregated. Perhaps because many Americans already stereotyped them as warriors, they were welcomed into the military and faced comparatively little discrimination.

The media's treatment of men and women in the military. On the left, the male branches reflect patriotism and the highest ideals. On the right, the woman is seen as a visual object, "just looking" until she can get out of uniform and back into fashion.

Meanwhile, more than 200 women Army nurses died in the line of duty, and 1,600 won combat and noncombat decorations such as the Purple Heart and the Distinguished Service Medal.

First Lady Eleanor Roosevelt (center) travels to college campuses to help recruit women students. With her are the directors of the WAVES, the WACS, and other groups. World War II was the first war to include women in the military in large numbers. Still, women's skills were often underutilized. They were assigned to clerical work, nursing, and other duties that would free men for combat. WAVES, for example, seldom got to leave the United States and were never assigned to combat duty; instead, they worked as gunnery instructors for men.

Of the 25,000 women who applied to the WASPS (Women's Air Force Service Pilots), only 1,830 were allowed to serve, and they were restricted to getting planes from factories to bases within the United States. The Navy refused to accept women.

Many girls on the home front idolized women in the service—they dressed up in their uniforms or had paper-doll WACS and WAVES. Such role models meant a lot to girls, who in neighborhood war games were usually relegated to the role of victim, or at most, nurse or spy.

ARMY AND NAVY MEDALS

NATIONAL DEFENSE SERVICE RIBBON
(A Medal Will Be Added After the War)

ARMY MEDAL OF HONOR

ARMY DISTINGUISHED SERVICE CROSS

ARMY DISTINGUISHED SERVICE MEDAL

ARMY SILVER STAR

ARMY PURPLE HEART MEDAL

ARMY SOLDIER'S MEDAL

ARMY AND NAVY DISTINGUISHED FLYING CROSS MEDAL

ARMY VICTORY MEDAL

NAVY MEDAL OF HONOR

NAVY DISTINGUISHED SERVICE MEDAL

NAVY CROSS

The highest awards given by the Army and Navy.
The fate of a combat soldier was unpredictable. Some served with distinction, performed acts of heroism, endured untold suffering—and emerged with medals for bravery.

Men on the Bataan Death March. Some soldiers fell into enemy hands and were taken prisoner. About 120,000 Americans were POWs during the war and subject to brutal treatment. Germany was known to treat American POWs comparatively well. Those POWs lost an average of thirty-eight pounds; 99 percent of them were eventually freed. The average American prisoner of the Japanese, however, lost sixty-one pounds, and only 73 percent survived.

In the most notorious example, 7,000 Americans and Filipinos died after being captured in the Philippines and forced to march the length of the thirty-mile Bataan peninsula to the Japanese POW camp. Most were killed after collapsing from starvation and lack of medical treatment for wounds.

An American soldier, wounded during a Japanese kamikaze attack aboard the USS Solace, being fed. One could also face serious injuries in battle, and many combat soldiers spent months in military hospitals. Disease and accidents sidelined even more, hospitalizing twenty-seven times more patients than did battle injuries. Two out of three soldiers with injuries eventually returned to battle.

Injuries could also be of the less visible kind—nervous conditions or combat fatigue. Men were three times more likely to suffer debilitating psychological symptoms than to be killed. The Army called these cases NP, for neuropsychiatric. The longer a battle went on, the greater the NP rate; during a month of fierce fighting in Italy, 54 percent of the American casualties were NP. Official photos never pictured soldiers afraid or crying—they were supposed to act tough and cool. But one study showed that during especially intense battles, one in four soldiers vomited, and one in ten wet their pants. Men who were able to keep fear from taking over their bodies reported being motivated by patriotism, bravery, and also kinship—a sense of not wanting to fail one's buddies.

Burial at sea, aboard the carrier Liscome Bay in 1943. The ultimate sacrifice, of course, was to lose one's life. Those in combat never knew if they would survive the day. Though the quality of medical care and medications had improved enormously in this century, the advances were offset by deadlier weapons and munitions. Therefore, battlefield death rates were about the same as in the Civil War.

The Sullivan brothers—Joseph, Francis, Albert, Madison, and George. The most famous example of sacrifice in combat was the Sullivans. After Pearl Harbor, all five rushed to enlist in the Navy, insisting that they remain together. Stationed aboard the USS *Juneau*, they were all killed when the ship was sunk in a battle off Guadalcanal in the South Pacific. The five were awarded posthumous Purple Heart medals. Their only remaining sibling, a sister named Genevieve, went on to join the WAVES.

The blue star (right) representing someone in service. Families with members in the military were entitled to hang plaques with a star in their window. The pride in this badge of honor helped to ease the anxiety families felt while waiting for loved ones to come home. The more members in the military, the more stars. A silver star meant that someone was wounded, and a gold star stood for a soldier who had died.

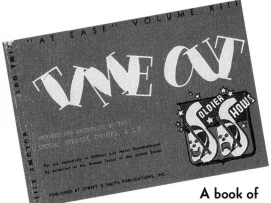

A book of games for soldiers. The military tried to relieve stress and take care of recreational needs. *Stars and Stripes*, the official Army newspaper, kept people informed and entertained. *Time Out* was the thirteenth volume in the "At Ease" series, distributed to armed forces passing the time or recuperating in hospitals. It included such games as "piddlydeewinx" (a version of tiddledywinks), "tire wrestling" (each wrestler standing inside a rubber tire), and "human croquet" (for sixteen men acting as balls and mallets). For more fun, there were mock debates to stage, on such topics as "the Army is better than the Navy" and whether "a wife should hold down a job or stay at home."

The Andrews Sisters—Maxine, Patty, and Laverne. Music was important to everyone. Many people even associate the whole war era with the Andrews Sisters, most famous for singing "Boogie Woogie Bugle Boy." The song that probably touched the most hearts was Irving Berlin's "I'm Dreaming of a White Christmas," as sung by Bing Crosby, for the memories it brought to soldiers far from home. Also popular was "I'll Be Home for Christmas," and its last line, "if only in my dreams."

A WAVE stationed in Clinton, Oklahoma, describes barracks pranks. "Everyone was in a rare mood," she writes, "and I don't think any of us got to sleep before 1 o'clock. We started out short-sheeting one of the girls and ended up doing just about everything we could think of." They even moved a woman's entire bed out on the front porch, then locked her outside in her pajamas while a bus full of sailors arrived.

Actor Mickey Rooney entertains the troops. Warfront USO (United Service Organization) shows, featuring the most famous performers from Broadway and Hollywood, were especially valuable in keeping up morale. Comedian Bob Hope was everywhere, racking up more travel time than any other performer.

Movie actresses Betty Grable, Carole Landis, Claudette Colbert, and Ruth Hussey (from left to right) surround two war heroes. Seated is Navy Ensign Donald Mason, reenacting the episode that resulted in his classic four-word radio message: "Sighted sub—sank same." Standing is Second Lieutenant George Welch, who shot down four Japanese planes at Pearl Harbor.

Mail was the serious morale booster during World War II. Those back home took their mission so seriously that each soldier received an average of fourteen pieces of mail a week. Sacks of mail were included on every ship and plane that left the United States. Any mail was a treat—except for a "Dear John" letter, in which a girlfriend would reveal she had fallen in love with someone else.

To cut costs, the government devised V-mail, a way of sending letters by microfilm. Officials on the receiving end enlarged and printed the negatives for delivery. Like all mail sent from the armed forces, V-mail was read by military censors, who excised any information (such as precise locations or troop movements) that could be dangerous if the letter fell into enemy hands. The seals on the upper left of these pieces of V-mail indicate that the messages had been approved by the censors.

An ensign stationed in the Pacific begs for more mail and describes a hard life: "We sleep in tents and must sleep with mosquito netting at all times. There is a great deal of malaria here. We're busy from 5 to 5 plus a four-hour watch every evening, seven days a week. I guess war is hell, isn't it?"

Mail was a way to bridge the gap between family members. This naval officer stationed in the southwest Pacific writes his mother: "So you really think that I am a different man than I used to be, do you? Well, it is quite possible, but maybe it is just that at last I am beginning to deserve the name 'man.'" He sends greetings to all his "lady friends," but seems to miss his mom most of all: "Goodby, sweetheart, and I'll be dreaming of you."

朝鮮俘虜收容所用箋

Dearest Jessie —

Sept 7, 1945.

Thank God it's all over at last. The war has been over three weeks but only today were we officially freed. Three American officers came into camp today and they promised to get this mail out by plane tomorrow. I have heard nothing from you in almost a year and a half and I pray to God that you and the babies have remained well through all this. I'm in relatively fit condition myself and expect to be with you in about a month. We will probably leave here by hospital ship tomorrow or next day — five days in Manila and then home — and you — I don't know if you have received any of my cards of the last few months, but I doubt it — I have been in Korea since April 27th — prior to that in Fukuoka Japan since Jan 31st — & prior to that a 6 week Hell trip from Manila, in which I was one of 300 survivors of an original sailing list of 1619 — You have no doubt, are listening to many horror stories now of Japanese atrocities toward war prisoners. They are all true. It is too good to be able now to write an uncensored letter but I prefer to wait and tell it to you in person — and soon —

The first thing this Army doctor does upon his release from a Japanese prisoner-of-war camp is to write to his wife: "Thank God it's all over at last...I have heard nothing from you in almost a year and a half [no mail having been delivered by the Japanese] and I pray to God that you and the babies have remained well...For 3 ½ years I haven't used a phone, heard a radio, used a flush toilet...I hope you haven't changed too much. I may have changed in many other ways, darling, but my love for you is unchanged. It's great to be an American, but it's greater still to be married to you."

43

In the years preceding World War II, Adolf Hitler gained control of Germany. The average German, having lost everything in World War I, was struggling to make ends meet. Money was literally worth less than the paper it was printed on; a postage stamp cost what a house had thirty years earlier. Four out of ten people had no job. Times were desperate, and Hitler claimed to have solutions.

In Europe, there was a long tradition of anti-Semitism, or hatred toward Jews. Their religion was different from that of Europe's Christian majority, and they were often made scapegoats when things went wrong. Hitler's own crusade was to convince Germany that, even though Jews made up less than 1 percent of the population, Jewish "domination" had somehow been responsible for Germany's loss in World War I. This belief was central to the formation of his political party—the National Socialist German Worker's Party, or Nazis.

"Holocaust" is the word commonly used for Nazi Germany's murder of an estimated six million European Jews during World War II. Derived from the Greek, meaning "burnt sacrifice," it refers to a time of "ethnic cleansing" on a massive scale—the ultimate expression of the dictatorship of Hitler.

Although by far the largest number of those killed were Jews, other victims included Soviet prisoners of war, Gypsies, the handicapped, homosexuals, Jehovah's Witnesses (and other pacifists), criminals, political prisoners, non-Jewish Poles (especially intellectuals), and even other Nazis if they departed from the party line. By the time Germany was forced to surrender to the Allies and the killing stopped, perhaps as many as 11 million people that Hitler considered undesirable were dead.

An American postcard mocking Hitler and his autobiography. *Mein Kampf* (*My Struggle*) was Hitler's blueprint for the future. In it, he described his belief that racial purity was the key to a nation's strength (Americans he dismissed as a "mongrel people") and that all "weaknesses" in the population had to be exterminated. White-skinned, blue-eyed blonds, which he called the Nordic, or Aryan, race, were the "master race" and thus had the right to rule. Non-Aryans were inferior, and those that lived in Eastern Europe, in particular, were meant to be slaves. Jews were the symbol of all evil. These ideas existed in Germany and other countries long before Hitler, but he argued vehemently that they had special application to Germany's current crisis.

While Americans hated Hitler, it was more for his aggression than for his policy toward Jews. Many around the world dismissed *Mein Kampf* as the work of a crackpot and did not take it seriously. But with Hitler's rise to power, it became the bible of Nazism and required reading for all Germans.

Hitler as the central attraction at a Nazi rally. Hitler carefully orchestrated his climb to the top with dramatic mass meetings and parades of followers chanting *"Sieg heil"* ("hail victory") and *"Heil Hitler"* ("hail Hitler"). In a time of confusion and despair, he accumulated power in part because he went after it so single-mindedly; others either underestimated him, or else were too unconcerned or self-interested to stop him.

By 1933, Hitler was in a position to make himself Germany's ruler, using *"Führer"* ("leader") as his title and calling his empire the "Third Reich." (The First had been the Holy Roman Empire, from 962 to 1806, and the Second had been

Otto von Bismarck's reign, from 1871 to 1890). It was intended to last a thousand years and make Germany the world's ruling power. Many German people adored Hitler; the sight of him could make both men and women cry. Three years into his reign, Germany became the only country with full employment. He had the support of the military and the business community, who were making money preparing for war. If some citizens noticed a loss of personal freedom and a more regimented life, it seemed a small price to pay for more jobs. Propaganda such as filmmaker Leni Riefenstahl's *Triumph of the Will* persuaded many that Hitler represented a brighter future.

Roll call of Hitler's private armed forces in 1935 (background). Hitler believed that possession of the streets was the key to power. His specially trained armies used force and intimidation to suppress opposition to the Third Reich. The SS (*Schutzstaffel*, or "protection squad") was originally Hitler's 280 bodyguards, but eventually became a private army of 250,000 tough, disciplined men—the most powerful organization in the Reich. Their motto was "Believe, Obey, Fight."

Thanks to the most feared branch of the SS—the Gestapo, or the Nazi State Secret Police—Hitler was able to further solidify his position by putting enemies into prisons. When the prisons grew too crowded, he ordered the building of concentration camps, where "undesirables" could be "concentrated" in one place and thus easily controlled.

As the symbol for Nazism, Hitler designed the swastika, a new version of a hooked cross, which like other crosses had been used as a good-luck symbol throughout history. The emblem is thought to derive from a 6,000-year-old Sanskrit word meaning "object of well-being" and has been found in pottery from ancient Baghdad, in Hindu temples, on Greek vases, and in American Indian art.

Members of Hitler Youth march in parade (background). Hitler had big plans for German children. When he began calling for members for his youth groups, as early as 1922, most kids found the idea appealing. It involved hiking trips to the countryside, camp-outs, competitions in all kinds of sports, war games, extra food rations, personal attention from *der Führer*, singing, and togetherness. By 1939, 82 percent (or seven million) of eligible youths in Germany belonged to Hitler Youth; it was the largest children's organization in the world. Its goal was to make the younger generation think exactly the way Hitler wanted them to think. Boys were to grow up to be good soldiers, and girls to be obedient wives and good mothers of more strong boys. The Hitler Youth motto for boys was "Live Faithfully, Fight Bravely, and Die Laughing!"; for girls it was "Be Faithful, Be Pure, Be German!"

There were no women in positions of Nazi leadership. Party doctrine held that women were inferior, except for their potential "childbearing achievement." Mothers who bore eight or more pure German children were awarded a gold Mother's Cross.

"Germans, defend yourselves! Do not buy from Jews!" reads this sign on a Jewish-owned business. The persecution of Jews was not a sudden development. The first omen of what was to come was a one-day boycott in 1933 of Jewish-owned businesses.

One month later, 200,000 books by such authors as Thomas Mann, Albert Einstein, Sigmund Freud, and other Jewish "undesirables" were set on fire in Berlin. Jews began to be banned from more and more places—theaters, libraries, beaches—and entire towns. Outside wooded areas were signs reading "Jews are not wanted in our German forests." The six-pointed Star of David was painted on Jewish-owned buildings. By 1941, all Jews could be easily identified by the yellow Star of David patch they were required to wear as a "mark of shame." New laws forbade them to vote and barred them from so many jobs that, by 1936, at least half the Jews in Germany had no way to make a living.

Anti-Semitic propaganda was broadcast on the radio,

and all classes in school were reorganized to fit Nazi theories. Kids studied charts of "Aryan" features (fair hair, narrow face and nose, light eyes, and white-pink skin) and were taught that people who looked this way were better than anyone else. Students learned a song that went, "Our Hitler is our lord, who rules a brave new world." The most popular children's board game in 1938, with over a million copies sold, was called "Get the Jews Out!" By that year, Jewish children were no longer allowed in public school.

Spectators look at a Jewish shop in Berlin, destroyed on Kristallnacht. On the night of November 9, 1938, a Polish Jew killed a minor German diplomat. Nazis seized on this as a pretext to riot. The riot marked a turning point, from repressive laws against Jews to organized violence. That night, the SS killed 91 Jews, arrested and beat up thousands more,  raped women, and burned over a thousand synagogues while crowds watched. They also wrecked 7,500 Jewish-owned stores, and the event took its name from the resulting damage—the Night of Broken Glass, or Crystal Night (*Kristallnacht*).

After this, Jews began to be sent to concentration camps in large numbers. The first of the many camps built throughout Germany and Eastern Europe was

Dachau, outside Munich. Each had a war business for which it used inmates as slave labor, under heavy guard and surrounded by electrified barbed-wire fences. "Extermination through work" was the initial policy—it was assumed that each worker would last an average of six weeks, given the camps' inhuman conditions, bad food, and lack of medicine.

All personal property was taken away, mostly for the benefit of the Nazis. Hitler had some religious artifacts sent to Prague, Czechoslovakia, where he planned to build the "Exotic Museum of an Extinct Race" after the war.

Jews who had not yet fled Germany were now willing to pay any price and undergo any danger to get out. But by the time the concentration camps were in full operation, the Jews were trapped, all roads of emigration closed.

Polish Jews being captured at gunpoint. As Hitler's forces began invading the rest of Europe, they rounded up Jewish families and forced them to live in isolated parts of towns. In these closed and guarded ghettos, approximately one-fifth of the residents eventually died of starvation and disease. This famous photograph was later used as evidence of Nazi brutality.

At this rate, Hitler estimated, it would take many years to clear Europe of Jews. There had to be a faster way. In 1939, he began experimenting with gas for mass killing during Operation T4, a program for ending "life unworthy of life"—the senile, deformed, retarded, incurably ill, invalids unable to work—some 250,000 people in all.

In 1942, Nazi leaders held a secret eighty-five-minute meeting in Wannsee, a Berlin suburb, to formalize what they called the "Final Solution to the Jewish Problem." Six death camps were hastily built whose only function was to kill Jews using Zyklon-B gas, which contained hydrocyanic acid, a lethal rat poison. All were in rural Poland, which had a long tradition of anti-Semitism and was far enough away for secrecy. The camps—Chelmno, Auschwitz-Birkenau, Belzec, Sobibor, Treblinka, and Maidanek—were not intended to last beyond their immediate purpose, and officials were careful to avoid spelling out what was happening, avoiding a "paper trail" that could be used against them later.

Starving children living behind barbed wire in the Buchenwald concentration camp, outside Weimar, Germany. As mass killing accelerated, prisoners in concentration camps had one of two fates: to be worked as slave labor, or to be killed immediately. The strongest were tattooed with blue numbers on their forearms and forced to work as long as they could live, while the elderly, the ill, and women with children were gassed. Most of the children under twelve, of less use as workers, were also killed.

In the ten years that Buchenwald was in operation, 70,000 people were murdered. The Nazis put 1,200 males, five to a bunk, into barracks meant to hold eighty horses. Every twenty-four hours, the prisoners received a small piece of brown bread and a tiny portion of stew.

American soldiers examining fake showerheads that had released gas in the chambers at one camp (right), and the ovens in which bodies had been burned after being gassed (bottom). As the end of the war neared, Nazis destroyed as much of the evidence as they could, including many of the camps. But enough remained behind to prove what had taken place.

After being forced to undress as if for bathing, prisoners were brought into a "shower room." There were no water pipes leading into these "showers," nor any drainage areas. The prisoners were locked inside, and the gas was turned on. Afterward, the bodies were burned.

Some German companies temporarily halted fighting the war and bid against each other for contracts to supply the ovens, ventilation systems, poisons, and other equipment necessary for this mass death. At Auschwitz-Birkenau, the largest camp, bodies were cremated at a rate of up to 2,200 a day in the camp's twelve ovens. With over 1.1–1.3 million people killed here—90 percent of them Jews—this camp is the world's largest cemetery.

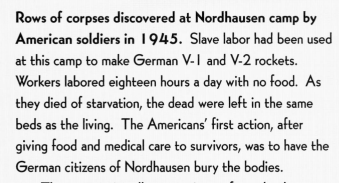

Rows of corpses discovered at Nordhausen camp by American soldiers in 1945. Slave labor had been used at this camp to make German V-1 and V-2 rockets. Workers labored eighteen hours a day with no food. As they died of starvation, the dead were left in the same beds as the living. The Americans' first action, after giving food and medical care to survivors, was to have the German citizens of Nordhausen bury the bodies.

There were virtually no survivors of any death camp except from Auschwitz-Birkenau and Maidanek, which were also concentration camps and slave labor camps. Between 60,000 and 100,000 people did survive the concentration camps—but just barely. To survive seemed to require the generosity of others, and many immeasurable strengths: a strong body, luck, the will to live, the ability to form attachments, a way of thinking of oneself first until one was in a position to help others, and an overriding desire to bear witness if Germany lost the war.

Some 20,000 survivors died in the first week after liberation, from weakness and disease.

Anne Frank, a symbol of the millions who were killed, especially children. Anne was a young German girl whose family had fled to Amsterdam, Holland. She had a beloved cat named Moortje, attended a Montessori school where she earned good grades except for math, and got in trouble for talking in class. Forced to go into hiding when Nazis began rounding up Dutch Jews, she and her family took refuge in the "Secret Annex," six hidden rooms in the building where her father's spice-importing business was located. They lived in confinement for more than two years. Anne passed the time by keeping up with homework, studying the pictures of movie stars she taped to her walls, and pouring her feelings into her diary.

Allied troops were on their way to Amsterdam when the Secret Annex group was betrayed by someone. Nazis found their hiding spot and sent the eight residents to Auschwitz-Birkenau and then to various other camps. Anne Frank died of typhus at the Bergen-Belsen concentration camp in March 1945, only two weeks before it was liberated by British troops. She was fifteen.

Oskar Schindler (second from right), surrounded by some of those he rescued. One of the most complex questions about World War II is how the rest of the world allowed the Holocaust to happen. Did no one try to stop it, or help the Jews escape?

In Germany, the majority of people seemed too passive, intimidated, or brainwashed by propaganda to help. They were being patriotic "good Germans" by going along with the Nazis.

The most famous exception was Oskar Schindler, a German Catholic businessman and member of the Nazi Party who personally saved the lives of 1,300 Jews. Risking his own life, he bribed and tricked the Nazis into sparing those who worked in his factories. There are more than 6,000 descendants of those he saved.

Elsewhere, a Swedish diplomat named Raoul Wallenberg saved thousands of Jews through direct and indirect means. In part due to him, Budapest had the only Jewish community of size left after the war—some 144,000. In Holland, the Bogaard family hid more than 300 Jews, many of them children, on their farm at various times. In Denmark, where anti-Semitism was almost unknown, the Danes smuggled almost their entire Jewish population of 7,000 across the sea to neutral Sweden to protect them from capture by Nazis in 1943.

How did the United States help? Between 1930 and 1941, some 25,000 mostly Jewish artists and scholars were able to flee to this country from Germany. But the United States, still reeling from the Depression, refused to accept more Jewish refugees. The ship *St. Louis*, for example, left Hamburg, Germany, in 1939 with 937 Jews, most with permits to land in America. When a presidential order forbade the ship from coming ashore, it cruised aimlessly for thirty-five days until several European countries agreed to share the refugees.

While the Holocaust was occurring, most Americans did very little. *Why* is still cause for speculation. Some of the indifference can be attributed to anti-Semitism. Also, many reports of atrocities during World War I had turned out to be false; when word of the concentration camps began to trickle out via eyewitnesses, it

KEEP the JAPS OUT of California

The only good Jap is dead

A plaque that some hung in their windows, demonstrating how much hatred existed in California. "The only good Jap is dead" was something military officers were heard to say, in an echo of an earlier era's dehumanization of American Indians.

Partly for the simple reason that they *looked* different from white Americans, popular culture was filled with propaganda about the "inscrutable Orientals"— nameless, faceless, all alike. Magazines ran articles like "How to Tell a Jap from a Chinese," about the physical details and traits that were supposed to distinguish the Japanese from our allies the Chinese. Restaurants hung signs that read "No Dogs or Japs Allowed."

A family has its car searched for evidence of disloyalty. As in most times of war, human rights began to suffer. The rights of Japanese-Americans, even when they were citizens, were gradually taken away. Japanese-Americans had to register with the government and were assigned numbers. An 8 P.M.–to–6 A.M. curfew was imposed on them. Some businesses refused to serve them.

A shop owner in Little Tokyo, Los Angeles, tries to protect himself by displaying as many signs of American patriotism as possible. In vain, Japanese-American business owners broadcast the truth—"I am an American." But their stores were still boycotted and sometimes vandalized. Filipino-Americans took to wearing buttons to distinguish themselves from America's enemies.

ASAHI DYE WORKS

朝日洋服洗濯所

FOR DEFENSE

GOD BLESS AMERICA

THIS PLACE OF BUSINESS IS OWNED AND OPERATED BY 100% AMERICAN CITIZEN OUR MOTTO VICTORY FOR AMERICA

BUY UNITED STATES SAVINGS BONDS AND STAMPS

USUAL

YOUR RED CRO

Camp Manzanar, the new home for many Japanese-Americans in California. In February 1942, President Roosevelt signed an order authorizing the evacuation of Japanese-Americans from the West Coast, where they were thought to pose the highest security risk. Lieutenant General John DeWitt, in charge of West Coast defense, was responsible for carrying out the order and establishing camps to house the evacuees. Hawaii was the only state where Japanese-Americans were not forced to relocate. They were a large percentage of the population there— not an easily intimidated minority—and their jobs were considered essential to the war.

Elsewhere, some 120,000 Japanese-Americans were uprooted from their lives, rounded up, and sent to one of ten relocation camps in California, Colorado, Utah, Arkansas, and other states.

With as little time as forty-eight hours to dispose of businesses, farms, and homes, they had to sell what they could and leave the rest behind. Stores that had displayed "I Am an American" signs now advertised "Going Out of Business" sales. Thousands of cats and dogs were left for humane societies to find.

Camp Manzanar, an Army barracks surrounded by swirling dust in the isolated California mountains, was a typical camp. All were located in rural areas or wastelands with harsh weather and bleak surroundings.

Some are taken to their new homes in trucks meant for cattle, wearing tags specifying their destination. Until the day of departure, the evacuees did not know where they were going.

Most evacuees went by train, like this crowd gathered with its belongings at a station. As much as the government tried to portray the evacuation as peaceful, almost voluntary, this photo demonstrates that armed military police were present to carry out the order.

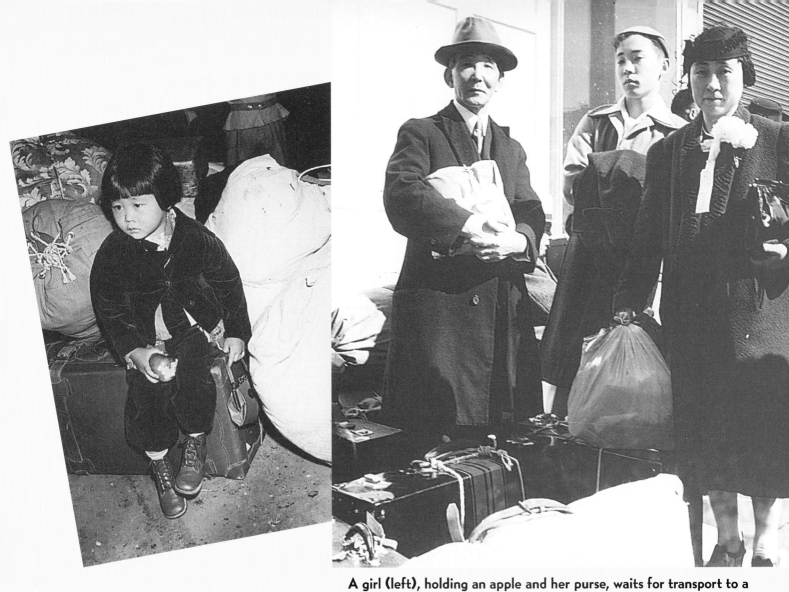

A girl (left), holding an apple and her purse, waits for transport to a camp. A fourteen-year-old boy (center), between his parents, is not as resigned to the situation as they seem to be. A small boy (right), in the process of being evacuated, still wears a "Remember Pearl Harbor" hat. The majority of evacuees were children, all classified as "enemies of the state." The government tried to depict Japanese-Americans as cheerful and stoic about the new arrangement, seeing it as a wartime necessity. Most people did cooperate without protest, believing that this sign of their loyalty to America would finally vindicate them. But the faces in photos tell a different story: of bewilderment, pain, betrayal, and worry.

The new housing was flimsy, barren, and crowded, with no privacy. No matter how prosperous their previous status, all evacuees now lived in the same conditions, with poor sanitation and no running water. Each family was assigned a small space, lit by a single bare lightbulb, with cots for beds, and shelves and furniture made from scrap lumber. Sometimes the internees had to build their own housing; or sometimes it was converted from abandoned race tracks or fairgrounds. Gates were locked and guarded twenty-four hours a day. The camps were officially called "War Relocation Centers" but were essentially prisons. Roosevelt himself once referred to them as concentration camps.

By June 1942, most of the 120,000 Japanese-Americans were living behind barbed wire.

Internment-camp school. Parents tried to make sure that children's lives went on as normally as possible. But kids were forced to study together despite their ages, with teachers who had been rejected for jobs elsewhere, using books cast off from other schools. School days began with pledging allegiance to the American flag.

Celebrating Christmas inside a prison camp.

The Hirano family, at the Colorado River Relocation Center, with a photograph of their son in the service. Some 33,000 Japanese-Americans served in the American armed forces. Some were drafted directly from the internment camps. Two of the most decorated units in the war were made up of Japanese-Americans.

As it turned out, no Japanese-American was ever convicted or even accused of spying or treason during World War II. Although putting them into camps violated at least five of the ten amendments in the Bill of Rights, most other Americans remained silent. Prejudice combined with ignorance—few even knew a Japanese-American person, especially once they had disappeared into camps.

After about a year, the interned were allowed to return home. All the camps were closed by 1944. For many, their old homes and farms had been destroyed; property and possessions that the government had promised to protect were gone. They received a tiny fraction of their estimated $400 million in total property losses. Meanwhile, the government had spent a total of $250 million on the relocation and support of the interned. In California, no one would hire them as farmworkers: the jobs had gone to Mexican-Americans as part of the *braceros* program that imported 30,000 Mexican railroad workers and farmworkers during the war. Most Japanese-Americans were in the same position as when their families had first come to the United States—starting from scratch. And the scars of such obvious persecution remained.

Chapter 7

PERSONALITIES:
WHO WAS WHO

The World War II era teemed with individuals who truly shaped history—amazing leaders who rose to whatever the occasion demanded of them, demonic villains responsible for unspeakable death and destruction, inspirational heroes, figures of enormous mystery and controversy. Here are a few of the personalities who seized the public imagination during the war.

The era's most dynamic hero was **FDR—Franklin Delano Roosevelt (1882–1945).** Born to a wealthy New York family, Roosevelt enjoyed a pampered childhood spent mostly in the company of adults. While he was a student at Harvard, his cousin Theodore Roosevelt became the twenty-sixth president of the United States. Franklin earned a law degree at Columbia University and went on to enter politics as a New York state senator. Later, he was elected governor. Defeating Republican President Herbert Hoover, Roosevelt became the thirty-second American president in 1932. His popularity was such that he was elected to an unprecedented four terms. Millions adored him, though some hated him and wouldn't even say his name (calling him "that man in the White House").

Roosevelt guided the United States through not one but two crises. His first term began during the height of the Depression, and in his first one hundred days he set about reviving the economy with programs and social reforms that became known as the New Deal. Policies that he developed, such as Social Security, continue to influence American life today.

In the middle of his second term, FDR entered into a confidential correspondence with British leader Winston Churchill. Their exchange of letters shaped Roosevelt's view of the danger Hitler's aggression posed to the world. When American isolationists prevented Roosevelt from declaring war, he supported Great Britain with the Lend-Lease Act, which enabled him to send money and supplies to help the Allies. By his third term, when the United States entered World War II, Roosevelt was a uniquely experienced president. As the nation's commander in chief, he directed its immense war effort, shaping national policy, coordinating the work of numerous government agencies, and holding conferences with the other Allied leaders.

Roosevelt was widely considered the most eloquent president since Abraham Lincoln. He worked hard on his speeches and delivered now-famous lines, such as "The only thing we have to fear is fear itself" (from his first inaugural address). During the war, many thought of themselves as fighting for the "four freedoms" he described in a 1941 speech: freedom of speech, freedom of every person to worship God in his or her own way, freedom from want, freedom from fear. Thanks to his innovative "fireside chats"—radio talks that brought him into living rooms as an intimate guest—people felt as if they knew him personally.

Roosevelt and his wife, Eleanor, relaxing at their six-hundred-acre farm in Hyde Park, New York, which they visited whenever they could. Their Scottish terrier, Fala, became the most famous and well-traveled dog of his day. Roosevelt was struck with polio at the age of thirty-nine and left permanently crippled. A rehabilitation center for polio victims in Warm Springs, Georgia, became his second home, which he visited for twenty years to get hot underwater massages. Photographs of Roosevelt rarely showed him in his wheelchair, and people tended to forget he couldn't stand up or walk without help. With his grand gestures, ready laugh, and contagious grin, he radiated confidence and energy. Winston Churchill once said that meeting him was like "opening a bottle of champagne."

Eleanor Roosevelt making a radio broadcast from the White House to promote the sale of war bonds.
Mrs. Roosevelt (1884–1962) was an important person in her own right, and certainly the first president's wife to have a public life and career.

She had lost her mother, father, and brother before the age of ten. For ten years after marrying FDR, her fifth cousin, in 1905, she was either having a baby or about to have one, and had most of the responsibility for their upbringing. Four of her sons served on active duty in the military during the war.

She and her husband were very different and led independent lives. In 1918, she learned that Roosevelt was having an affair with her secretary. Rather than divorce him (which would have ruined his political career), she decided to stand by him. During the war, she visited troops, traveling as much as 23,000 miles a year. Her earnings from writing and teaching usually topped her husband's income (she gave them to charity). Her newspaper column, "My Day," was the most widely read feature in the United States.

After Franklin's death, she became one of the first five American delegates to the United Nations and hosted a weekly TV interview show. She was also the world's foremost spokesperson for human rights, a champion of the rights of children and of civil rights for American blacks. She also threw her influence into attempts to allow more Jewish refugees into the United States, but with no success. She died at age seventy-eight after a stroke—the most famous, admired, and influential woman of her time.

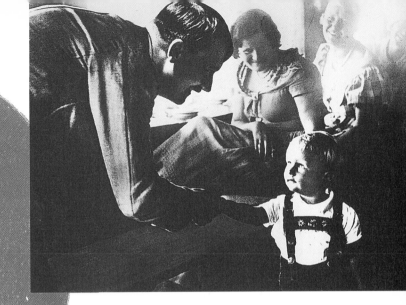

Adolf Hitler smiles at a young German boy, in a photo distributed throughout Germany as a postcard labeled "A Child's Gaze." Hitler (1889–1945) probably had more impact on the world than any other person in this century. Anxious to be seen as a father figure, he became in fact the most disruptive and hated figure of World War II.

Hitler's grandmother worked as a maid in a Jewish household, and his grandfather may have been Jewish. His father was harsh and irritable, their clashes were explosive, and Hitler was whipped every day as a boy.

He dreamed of being a great artist, but was rejected by art schools. He spent his time reading, taking long walks by the river, and selling his pictures when he could. At times, he lived on the streets. He loved music, especially the operas of Richard Wagner, with their vision of a Germany glorious in its past and future.

During World War I, Hitler was twice decorated for bravery in the Army before being temporarily blinded by chlorine gas. He swore that if he regained his sight he would enter politics and avenge Germany's humiliating surrender. Sight restored, he led an unsuccessful revolt and spent nine months in prison for treason. The publicity turned him into a national leader, and upon his release he began an eight-year direct march to power.

Heard in person by an estimated 35 million people in all, Hitler was said to have been one of the most magnetic speakers in history. He would begin haltingly, but over the course of several hours become so fiery that he could lose up to five pounds a night in sweat. Some people fainted from emotion or claimed they saw a halo around his head. After surviving several assassination attempts, he became convinced he was infallible, destined to rule the world.

Those who worked for Hitler realized that he was unstable. He was famous for unpredictable rages, and no one wanted to be a target. A hypochondriac who kept two doctors with him most of the time, Hitler was a health-food fanatic except for a weakness for rich pastries. He was a vegetarian, didn't drink or smoke, and had no friends.

By 1943, he was dependent on narcotics and stimulants to combat depression and nervous ailments. As the war went against him, he retained an unshakable belief in himself, but became increasingly secluded in his underground bunker headquarters, protected from the outside world by twenty-six feet of concrete.

On April 29, 1945, Hitler married his mistress of fifteen years, Eva Braun, in a ceremony within the bunker. It fulfilled her dearest wish, made their relationship "respectable" in society—and perhaps compensated her for what was to follow the next day (see page 81).

Joseph Goebbels (1897–1945), Germany's minister of public enlightenment and propaganda. He determined what Germans were told; everything in print, as well as movies and the arts, had to pass his censorship. Though pockmarked, tiny, and affected by a bad limp (he weighed less than a hundred pounds and had a clubfoot from a bout with childhood polio), Goebbels was a charismatic speaker, second in popularity to Hitler. His six children called Hitler "Uncle Führer." On April 30, 1945, with Germany's defeat imminent, Goebbels and his wife, Magda, took cyanide after she had poisoned the children—Helga, Hilde, Helmut, Holde, Hedda, and Heide.

Others in the Third Reich who helped Hitler carry out his plans included grossly fat Hermann Goering (1893–1946), who founded and headed the Gestapo, rejuvenated the German Air Force, and stole some $200 million worth of paintings from European collections. Unimposing Heinrich Himmler (1900–45) was chief of the SS, later minister of the interior, and established the first concentration camp. Reinhard Heydrich (1904–42) was one of the few Nazi leaders who actually looked like the Aryan ideal, but in fact he had Jewish ancestors. Hitler and Himmler used their knowledge of this to force him to prove his loyalty—they gave him the authority to carry out the Final Solution. Heydrich set about exterminating Jews with extraordinary thoroughness and was himself killed when his car was bombed by the Czech Resistance. In retaliation, the Nazis destroyed the town of Lidice in Czechoslovakia, killed all of its inhabitants, and took its name off the map. In memorial, towns in Illinois, New York, and Mexico changed their names to Lidice.

Rudolf Hess, as Hitler's personal secretary, was so loyal that he once intercepted a beer mug thrown at Hitler—and bore a permanent scar on his forehead. Later, Martin Bormann replaced him as Hitler's right-hand man, eventually becoming the most powerful and feared man after Hitler. Bormann translated Hitler's rambling verbal directions into writing and acted as Hitler's shadow, supplying everything from special food to reading material.

Hirohito, the emperor of Japan, astride his favorite horse, Shiroutuka. Hirohito (1901–89) was an ordinary-looking man with six children, passionate about marine biology, shy and retiring. But as emperor he was presumed to be descended from gods and goddesses, infallible and all-powerful. The Japanese believed that looking at the emperor directly would make you blind and that the most sacred thing was to die for him. His commands came via advisers, who as humans could be blamed for giving him false advice.

Hirohito began his reign by calling it *Showa*, or "Bright Peace," and often expressed himself in haiku, or seventeen-syllable poems. His policy of not issuing direct orders—"reigning, not ruling"—allowed his military advisers to push the country into aggressive expansion, then war. There are no records indicating whether Hirohito approved of the war or not. One of his few reactions was to recite a poem from his grandfather: "All the seas, everywhere,/are brothers one to another/Why then do the winds and waves of strife/rage so violently through the world?" During the war, he lost twenty pounds after limiting himself to the rations his subjects were given. His wife, the Empress Nagako, wrote letters to each of the parents of the war dead.

At the end of the war, Hirohito was influential in getting Japan to accept unconditional surrender and helping the country back on its feet. He renounced his belief in imperial divinity and had all of his powers taken away, except for ceremonial ones. He died of cancer and was buried with some of his favorite possessions: a microscope, a listing of sumo wrestlers, and a Mickey Mouse watch given to him on a visit to Disneyland.

General Hideki Tojo, prime minister of Japan (1884–1948). The most important of the "Big Six"—the advisers who made all the decisions in wartime Japan—Tojo issued commands in the emperor's name and became a totalitarian dictator in the manner of Hitler. As Americans began to suspect that Hirohito was not giving the orders, Tojo was understood to be in control and as a result became much hated.

Nicknamed "the Razor" for his shrewd, decisive manner, Tojo had a shrill voice and was dour and bald. His job was his life. He had no hobbies, no friends, and no time for his wife, Katsuko, or their seven children. After he was blamed for Japan's losses in the war and forced to resign in the summer of 1944, he had nothing to do but work in his garden. Surrender was unthinkable. Even after the atomic bombs had been dropped on Japan, Tojo intended to spend his retirement underground, living in a cave with his family, coming out only to forage for sweet potatoes.

Once Japan did surrender, many of its leaders committed suicide. Tojo shot himself, but survived. He was tried by an international tribunal as a war criminal for conspiracy to wage aggressive war and for atrocities against POWs, and was executed in 1948.

Benito Mussolini, the Italian dictator, striding in a 1943 parade. Mussolini (1883–1945), leader of Italy for twenty-one years, was the third-most-hated person in the United States after Hitler and Tojo. Nicknamed *Il Duce* ("the Leader"), he founded the National Fascist Party. He even coined the term *fascism* (from *fascio*, Italian for "bundle of sticks"; it symbolized that a single stick breaks easily, but a bundle together is strong). Fascism was a way of government that glorified a nation and an authoritarian ruler at the expense of the individual. Mussolini allied himself with Germany, though he privately considered Hitler's ideas "incoherent."

Even as a teen on the school playground, Mussolini had drawn crowds when voicing opinions on politics or religion. Educated as an elementary-school teacher, he became a highly theatrical speaker. He had costumes with hats for each of the various roles he took in government, and he shaved his head for effect.

A fitness fanatic, he left his duties only for strenuous exercise (riding, boxing, fencing). He hated overindulgence and ate and drank little. He had five children with his wife, Rachele, and others with other women.

As the Allies prepared to invade Italy, some Fascists revolted aginst Mussolini. After the German surrender, he and his lover, Clara Petacci, were captured by rivals and executed. His last words were "Shoot me in the chest."

Tojo, Hitler, and Mussolini are mercilessly ridiculed in the United States. In this tire company's ad, motorists were urged to drive below forty miles per hour to save wear on tires—going any faster would only give satisfaction to the Axis.

Axis leaders represented Evil and gave many American kids nightmares. But the leaders were also a source of ironic amusement, as in the chant, "Whistle while you work,/Hitler is a jerk,/Mussolini is a weenie/And Tojo is a jerk."

Winston Churchill, England's prime minister, smiles victoriously on his way to Parliament to announce the Allied landings in France on June 6, 1944. One of the war's great heroes, Churchill (1874–1965) had already had a distinguished political career when the war began. First elected to Parliament in 1900, he served as First Lord of the Admiralty during World War I.

Out of office between 1929 and 1939, he issued unheeded and unpopular warnings about Germany's aggression and the inevitability of war. In 1938, he bitterly opposed the Munich Pact, signed by then Prime Minister Neville Chamberlain, Hitler, and Mussolini, which gave large areas of Czechoslovakia to Germany. Churchill believed that this policy of "appeasement" only eased the way toward Hitler's conquest of Europe. The next year he was again appointed First Lord of the Admiralty. After the Nazis went on to invade the Netherlands, Chamberlain resigned, and Churchill took over as prime minister and minister of defense at age sixty-six: "At last I had the authority to give directions over the whole scene," he wrote later. Knowing that Britain could not defeat Germany on its own, he began doing everything in his power to persuade the United States to enter the war with him.

Britain was the only non-neutral European country not to fall to Hitler, due in large part to the enormously popular Churchill. His leadership was fearless and indefatigable. "We shall defend our island, whatever the cost may be," he declared, rallying people

to heroic sacrifice. "We shall fight on the beaches. We shall fight on the landing grounds. We shall fight in the fields and the streets. We shall fight in the hills. We shall never surrender!"

A flamboyant, inspirational speaker, Churchill had a way with words. Trying to predict Russia's role in the war, he called the country "a riddle wrapped in a mystery inside an enigma." Nazism was "the foulest and most soul-destroying tyranny which has ever darkened and stained the pages of history." Churchill also had a distinguished writing career, and in 1953 won the Nobel Prize in literature for his six-volume war memoirs.

After the war, his popularity decreased, and he was voted out. In 1951, opinion changed again, and he became prime minister once more. After deciding to resign at the age of eighty, he spent his retirement painting. He died ten years later.

Josef Stalin (1879–1953), Russian revolutionary and head of the Soviet Union. Little is known about Stalin's childhood, because he had almost everyone who knew him then killed.

He was born Joseph Djugashvili, son of a poor shoemaker who beat him so severely that he was seldom seen without a black eye. A bruise on one arm developed blood poisoning and caused the arm to stay three inches shorter than the other, lame and useless. After his first wife died of tuberculosis, he claimed that any warm feeling he had for people had died with her. He took the name "Stalin," which meant "Man of Steel." His second wife committed suicide in 1932 during their unhappy marriage. He was anti-Semitic and refused to meet five of his eight grandchildren because they were part Jewish.

After becoming the ruler of the largest country in the world in 1924, Stalin transformed the Soviet Union into a superpower, forcing the press, people, and industries to obey his commands. "A single death is a tragedy," he said, "a million deaths is a statistic." During his reign of terror, fourteen million peasants died as a result of a famine he created with artificial food shortages. His secret police killed between seven and nine million more in a "purge" of the

disloyal. They were either executed or imprisoned to die a lingering death as slave labor. He built the world's largest prison system in remote locations like Siberia, where the temperature could fall to 104 degrees below zero.

Stalin's own greatest fear was assassination. He was surrounded by thousands of guards, and had all his food chemically analyzed before he ate it.

During the war, Stalin put policy ahead of people. Soviet troops were ill-trained and unprotected, and when men were taken as POWs by Germany, Stalin denounced them as traitors and did nothing to rescue them. Thousands of the country's towns and villages were destroyed by invading armies, and 38 percent of all the deaths in World War II were Russian.

After the war, Stalin began to seal the country off and teach Russians to hate anything foreign. He repaired the war damage, expanded industry, and created "satellite" communist states in Eastern Europe as barricades against the democracies. Within fifteen to twenty years, he planned to take over the rest of the world by initiating World War III. But he died of a stroke eight years into his plan, at age seventy-four.

General Charles de Gaulle, president of the French Provisional Government, after his triumphal entry into Paris. De Gaulle (1890–1970) was a decorated infantry officer in World War I, and by 1939 was the youngest general in the French Army. Like millions around the world, he opposed France's surrender to Germany the following year. He flew to London to join the European heads of state in flight from the Nazis. For this he was condemned to death for treason by Vichy France, the new French government authorized by Germany (named for its capital at Vichy, a famous French spa).

Remaining in London, de Gaulle created Free France, a government that was ready to take over as soon as the Germans were forced to retreat. "I am France!" he said, declaring himself the legitimate leader of Free France. Because he acted so independently, de Gaulle was controversial among the Allies. But he supplied a steady source of hope to the French Resistance movement during the four years of Nazi occupation, and his personal bravery was legendary. His reward came in the form of jubilant cheers once Paris was liberated in 1944. At the start of Operation Overlord (see p. 78), de Gaulle had insisted that his government be recognized, and when French and American troops entered Paris, de Gaulle was with them. For collaborating with the Nazis, Vichy officials were condemned to death or dishonor.

De Gaulle later became president of France from 1959 to 1969. One year after leaving office, he died at age eighty.

Dwight D. Eisenhower (1890–1969), the most popular American military hero to come out of World War II. A Kansas farm boy from Abilene, Eisenhower was more famous at West Point for football and poker than for his military ambitions. At forty-nine, he was an obscure lieutenant colonel who had never seen combat. Then the war began, and the likable Eisenhower won promotion to chief of Army operations in Washington, D.C., and then to U.S. commander of the European theater of operations. In 1943, Roosevelt appointed him supreme commander of Allied forces, and Eisenhower proceeded to lead the Allies to victory in Europe. His success at coordinating and directing Operation Overlord transformed his image into the ultimate crusader against Nazi evil. He would later become the thirty-fourth president of the United States (see p.94). A popular leader, he was always self-confident and cheerful, with the philosophy that victory is a result of optimism spreading downward from the commander. He hated war and felt the emotion of loss deeply.

During the war, Eisenhower wrote over a hundred letters a year to his wife, Mamie. When he died at age seventy-nine, his last words were, "I've always loved my wife. I've always loved my children. I've always loved my grandchildren. And I have always loved my country."

General Douglas MacArthur (1880–1964), commander in chief of the Pacific theater, with his trademark corncob pipe and sunglasses. During his career, "Mac" probably earned more medals than anyone in American history: twenty-two—thirteen of them for heroism. The Army was his whole life; even his wife addressed him as "General." Although Roosevelt ordered him out of the Philippines to Australia, MacArthur never lost sight of his goal to come back: "I shall return," he said, in the most famous promise in American military history. And he did. In the Battle of Leyte Gulf, a major Philippine triumph, the Japanese lost 10,000 men. It was one of the biggest naval battles of all time.

People had strong feelings about MacArthur. He was tactless and pompous and loved publicity, with a theatrical streak that annoyed many. Others worshiped him for imposing total surrender on Japan against heavy odds. After the war, babies, streets, and dances were named after him.

After directing the postwar occupation of Japan, MacArthur was removed from command during the Korean War by President Truman. He died at age eighty-four from kidney and liver failure.

Private First Class Ira Hayes, age nineteen, ready to jump while at the Marine Corps Paratroop School. As one of the six Marines photographed at the Iwo Jima flag-raising amid heavy fire (see p. 83), Hayes (1922–1955) became a national hero. The photo created enormous publicity, and Hayes became a star attraction at war-bond rallies. A full-blooded Pima Indian, he also symbolized the hopes of American Indians but encountered stereotyped attitudes constantly. His nickname was "Chief Falling Cloud."

Hayes was described by one who knew him as "a hero to everyone but himself." A modest person who didn't like the pressure of being in the spotlight, he died from alcoholism at age thirty-three on an Arizona reservation. He received a lavish military funeral and was buried at Arlington National Cemetery.

J. Robert Oppenheimer, the brilliant director of the Manhattan Project—the United States' plan to build an atomic bomb. An American Jew, with friends and relatives in Germany, Oppenheimer (1904-1967) believed Hitler would return Western civilization to the Dark Ages. Many of the scientists, notably Albert Einstein, who were important to the development of the atomic bomb were Jews who had fled to the United States from Germany years earlier.

Oppenheimer, a professor at the University of California at Berkeley, had two great passions—physics and the desert scenery of New Mexico. As the Manhattan Project's director, he arranged for its center to be built in Los Alamos, New Mexico. It was the largest building ever constructed, for the most expensive ($2 billion) science project in the history of the world. Oppenheimer oversaw six hundred people working around the clock to build a bomb before the Nazis could; participants were subject to a $10,000 fine and ten years in prison for talking about what they were doing. The site was so secret it had no address.

After the war, most Americans thought the atomic bomb played a decisive role in ending it; Oppenheimer became a celebrity and was asked to run for office. But he had doubts. "Physicists have known sin, and this is knowledge they cannot lose," he said. He wanted to prevent the military from abusing the bomb and opposed development of the hydrogen bomb. (President Truman proceeded with it anyway.)

This, plus his communist associations (his wife, Kitty, was a member of the Communist Party), was used against Oppenheimer. In the 1950s, he was suspected of being a Russian spy. Being declared a national security risk destroyed him, and he never worked for the government or in nuclear energy again.

Harry S Truman, making his first speech to Congress as president in April 1945. After Roosevelt's sudden death (see p. 81), Vice President Truman (1884-1972) succeeded him. He became president at a critical moment—the final four months of the war—taking over its coordination from his extremely popular predecessor. Truman was the one who, in trying to force Japan to surrender, made the decision to drop the atomic bomb. He made numerous other tough decisions throughout his presidency. For a time, he had on his desk in the White

House a sign that said "The Buck Stops Here." Peppery and plainspoken, he was known as "Give-'em-Hell Harry."

He later won an election on his own, and played an important role in establishing Israel, helped to create the United Nations and the Central Intelligence Agency, and desegregated the military.

Truman had no education beyond high school, but was an avid reader all his life. His wife, Bess, and daughter, Margaret, could not recall seeing him at home without a book in his hand. He died at age eighty-eight.

Chapter 8

WEAPONS,
DIRECT AND INDIRECT

World War I battles had been fought in trenches with the rapid-firing machine gun; World War II warfare was most famous for bombs and bombers. Military leaders had seen that ground forces suffered the most casualties, and they were anxious to find alternatives to bloody land campaigns.

Countries raced each other to develop new weapons, but not all of the experiments were successful. One notable American "failure" was the attempt to design a weapon that would kill by focusing radio waves on a target. This turned into a success as something else: radar, a way of using radio to "see" at night.

Numerous new methods of fighting in the air, on land, and on sea were born. Besides the direct means of bombs and torpedoes, there were also sophisticated ways of fighting indirectly, behind the scenes.

And although there was a civilian fascination with the weapons of war, the reality was that these were a means of killing.

A German V-1 buzz bomb in flight (background). In the race to invent new weapons, Germany took an early lead. Hitler and his wizard of rocketry, Wernher von Braun, intended their "V for Vengeance" missiles to be the "decisive weapons of the war." The V-1 missile, or pilotless plane, was the world's first guided missile. It was stuffed with explosives, powered by buzzing jet engines, and launched from a catapult. The most frightening moment was when the buzz would stop—that meant the bomb was about to fall and strike at random. During one nine-month period in 1940, 2,420 of the V-1 bombs hit London, killing more than 6,000 civilians.

The V-2 rocket was more deadly and sophisticated, the precursor of today's missiles. It flew at 3,600 miles per hour, too fast for any interception, and arrived without warning. It had no weakness except one: it cost ten times as much to produce as the V-1.

The only defense against the V-2 was to destroy the German manufacturing and launch sites. Not until almost the end of the war were the Allies able to overtake the last of the launching pads.

Chapter 9

One of the United States military cemeteries in France—La Cambe, established two days after D-Day. The many military cemeteries on the coast of France underscore the human cost of the Allied victory. In the first twenty-four hours after D-Day, thousands died or were wounded under heavy Nazi machine-gun fire. In the last six months of 1944, between 12,000 and 18,000 GIs were dying each month. Over 4,500 Americans are buried at La Cambe.

Churchill, Roosevelt, and Stalin at Yalta. With Germany on the brink of collapse, the leaders of the "Big Three" countries (the United States, Great Britain, and the Soviet Union) held a meeting in February 1945. At Yalta, a city in Russia, they prepared the groundwork for postwar Europe, including the terms for Germany's surrender. After the war, Germany was to be divided into four zones occupied by the United States, the Soviet Union, Great Britain, and France.

Two months later, in the midst of worldwide turmoil, Roosevelt dies in Warm Springs, Georgia, April 12, 1945. During his fourth term, with his health failing, he suffered a stroke. His last words were "I have a terrific headache." Americans had a new leader, Vice President Harry S Truman, to take over at this crucial time.

Two weeks after Roosevelt's death, Mussolini is executed by Italian opponents. Soon after, Hitler is dead at age fifty-six. As these headlines indicate, the cause of Hitler's death on April 30, 1945, was not immediately clear. So many people were trying to kill Hitler by this point that it was first thought he had been assassinated. But in fact he shot himself in a double suicide with Eva Braun, who took poison. His grand delusions remained intact; in one of his last speeches, he said, "We are going to destroy everybody who does not take part in the common effort for the country."

But German defeat was now certain, and Hitler refused to give the Allies the satisfaction of taking him prisoner. Nor did he want his body to be found and used as a war trophy. After their deaths, he and Braun were immediately cremated. Numerous Nazi leaders followed them in suicide.

A week later, Germany surrenders. The surrender took place on May 7 in a little red schoolhouse—Eisenhower's headquarters at Reims, France. Instead of lasting a thousand years, the Third Reich had lasted twelve.

In the United States, May 8 was declared V-E Day—Victory in Europe Day. Truman urged Americans not to celebrate just yet. After all, the war was only half-won.

American soldiers ride tanks into liberated Paris, along the Champs Élysées, its most famous boulevard. The fall of Paris in 1940, at the zenith of Hitler's power, had stunned the world. The longer the war had lasted, the more lives were being lost. New evidence was indicating that had the Germans been able to hold out another year—which could easily have happened—they would have mass-produced new weapons, with ever more deadly consequences. Now the sight of American Sherman tanks—bringing candy and gum, not gunfire—was so welcome that tears streamed down many Parisians' faces.

Victorious United States Marines raising the American flag at Iwo Jima. Once victory in Europe was close at hand, the Allies could pour all their energies into defeating Japan. An island-by-island campaign began in the central Pacific. Each captured island on the way toward Japan was a jumping-off place for the next capture. Believing in death before dishonor, Japanese soldiers fought back with no concern for their own lives.

The ferocious struggle for the island of Iwo Jima came to symbolize American heroism and devotion to duty: one-third of all the Marines killed in the Pacific died here. The photo recording the moment of victory on February 23, 1945, seems to show war as a collective effort that also recognizes individuals.

The closer the Americans got to Japan, the harder the Japanese fought. The capture of Okinawa became the last major battle of the Pacific war and one of the costliest. By June 21, 1945, some 12,500 Americans were dead and many more wounded in a battle that was supposed to take forty-five days, but took eighty.

The United States dropped 19 million pamphlets on forty-seven Japanese cities urging a surrender, and a blockade was in effect that had most civilians near starvation. Japanese schools were closed so that students could grow food, gather firewood, and train for the army. A volunteer army was mobilizing all available women and men from ages thirteen to sixty.

Mushroom cloud created when the United States dropped the atomic bomb on Hiroshima in August 1945 (background). As the war dragged on in Japan, President Truman and other leaders were appalled at rapidly rising American death rates. General MacArthur estimated that one million American lives would be lost if Japan had to be invaded, the most likely next step. To forestall this extremely unpopular prospect, Truman authorized the dropping of two atomic bombs on Japan.

The first bomb (nicknamed "Little Boy") plummeted from the Superfortress *Enola Gay*, piloted by Colonel Paul Tibbets, at 8:15 A.M. on August 6. The target was the city of Hiroshima. With a power equal to 15,000 tons of TNT, the explosion created a cloud that rose 40,000 feet and a fireball that was 1,800 feet across and had a center temperature of 100 million degrees. In nine seconds, it killed 66,000 people outright. In all, it killed an estimated 100,000, and erased an area about four miles square. Some 62,000 out of 90,000 buildings were destroyed, with many more damaged beyond repair.

Remains of the Nagasaki Medical College, with tree damage in the foreground. Three days later, the second bomb (nicknamed "Fat Man") was dropped on Nagasaki by Major Charles Sweeney from a B-29 named *Bock's Car*. The only buildings left after the bombing were of reinforced concrete; all suffered varying degrees of damage.

American military leaders had decided to drop the bombs on Japanese cities relatively untouched by the recent B-29 carpet bombing, and had spared some cities for just this purpose. Only four cities qualified—Hiroshima, Kyoto, Kokura, and Niigata. The industrial city of Nagasaki was a last-minute possibility, added when Kokura was obscured by clouds on the designated day.

Nagasaki victim. During the two blasts, people were instantly vaporized. Many thousands more were wounded, with burned skin and radiation sickness that caused them to vomit and die within days. Just before Hiroshima was bombed, hundreds of schoolgirls had been put to work clearing fire lanes, preparing for air raids. They were out in the open when the bomb hit. The few who survived were badly scarred and became known as the A-Bomb Maidens.

Others who survived were stigmatized as *hibakusha*, or "explosion-affected persons." Their children suffered birth defects, and they could not get jobs because employers knew they were prone to many diseases, especially leukemia and other cancers. Radiation killed for years to come; American scientists had greatly underestimated its effects.

The decision to use the atomic bombs will be forever debated. Truman hoped that this greatest possible shock to Japan would change its militant stance and force it to surrender, saving American lives. And indeed, on August 14, Emperor Hirohito announced, "I cannot bear to see my innocent people suffer any longer." The war was over.

At the time, a poll showed that 85 percent of Americans approved of the use of the atomic bombs. As more information came out about the ferocity of the destruction, though, this percentage declined.

Allied soldiers and sailors look on as Japanese Foreign Minister Mamoru Shigemitsu signs surrender documents on September 2, 1945, in Tokyo Bay. Moments after MacArthur signed on behalf of the Allies, his voice came over a microphone: "A great victory has been won. The skies no longer rain death—the seas bear only commerce—men everywhere walk upright in the sunlight. The entire world is quietly at peace."

In Japan, a thousand military officers and hundreds of civilians committed suicide, many in a plaza before the ruins of the emperor's Imperial Palace, where the blood ran for days.

Two million people surge into Times Square (right), the heart of New York City, to rejoice. In the United States, V-J Day—Victory over Japan Day—was announced in the early evening of August 15.

Ecstatic celebrations lasted all night. Truman declared a two-day holiday, and all across the United States, streets jammed with crying, laughing, shouting people. Many people ducked into churches to say a prayer of thanks. Kids ran into the streets in pajamas for hugs and conga dances. For some kids, it was the most memorable day of the war, like one gigantic New Year's Eve celebration.

Kissing seemed the natural thing to do that night, in one of the war's most famous photographs. Home-front women all wanted to kiss men in uniform, and many people got their first kiss on V-J Day.

Mourning the dead on the Ryukyu Islands in the Pacific. The end of the war was a time to reflect on this, the bloodiest, costliest war in history. It had left an estimated 60 million people dead, two-thirds of them civilians— mostly women and children. Several times that number were physically or psychologically disabled. Some received no burial. On July 29, 1945, just after delivering a vital part of the atomic bomb from San Francisco to the Japanese island of Tinian, the USS *Indianapolis* was ripped apart by Japanese torpedoes. Because of miscommunication, no one in the Navy realized the ship was missing. For four full days, the survivors were alone in the ocean, with life rafts—and sharks. Out of the crew of 1,199, only 316 men survived. The *Indianapolis* was to be the last American ship sunk by the enemy during World War II.

The "Asakusa Higashi-

新宿

"...ji Temple," converted into a home for the homeless.

...ig store.

Millions of Europeans and Asians are now homeless. The war had destroyed more property than any other in history. Major cities across Europe lay in ruins, with priceless architecture and artwork smashed, and one person out of four without shelter. In the Soviet Union, many thousands lived in hillside dugouts or bombed-out cellars for as long as three years after the war.

In Japan, all the major cities were unlivable wastelands, with 13 million people homeless. People lived in cars and burned-out buildings, with almost no food except acorns.

89

A wounded GI gets a homecoming in August 1945 from a daughter he has never seen. Meanwhile, American soldiers were returning to ticker-tape parades and marching bands that honored them as heroes.

But many did not come home. Besides the 670,846 that were wounded, and the countless others who were emotionally scarred, World War II left 405,399 mostly young Americans dead.

A serviceman reunites with his wife while their child looks for attention.
War's end was, of course, an enormous relief, but it was not always "happily ever after." For kids especially, reunions could be difficult. Those who had never met or really known their father worried that he'd fail to recognize them. Mothers had built up dads as superheroes, and the dads didn't necessarily live up to the image. Sometimes they attempted to impose the sort of discipline they learned in the military, and kids rebelled. Kids were used to living in families of women, and just hearing a man's voice, especially in anger, was strange for some.

Fathers had been changed by their war experiences. And women were not the same people the men had left; *their* war experiences had made them stronger. Conflict was inevitable.

Popular media make light of the problems of returning American soldiers, as if their most serious challenge is learning to diaper their babies. But the truth was that all had some kind of readjustment problem—whether financial, psychological, or professional. Emotional difficulties ranged from loneliness and depression to alcoholism and mental disorders. Children remember their fathers being very nervous, intolerant, distant. Men were unsure how to fit back into families that seemed complete without them. World War II had been hard on family life. Its end was a blessing, to be sure; but for some families, it was a mixed one.

The Family Circle MAGAZINE

SOME LASTING EFFECTS
OF WORLD WAR II

Like a big rock dropped into a pond, World War II caused endless ripples that continue up to the present day. Some of its effects extend or conclude several stories in this book.

✪ World War II left the United States in a uniquely powerful position. Never invaded or heavily bombed, it was able to dramatically increase its manufacturing. By 1946, with less than 6 percent of the world's population, the United States was producing almost half the world's products (compared to one-quarter by the 1990s). Now the richest and most powerful nation in the world, it was the only major power to emerge from the war stronger than before. Americans had learned new skills in wartime jobs and expanded their options. More people took an interest in world events and lost their isolationist attitude; certainly, they never wanted to get caught unprepared again. No longer preoccupied with itself, the United States had become the "Leader of the Free World." Indeed, it was from this point on even considered "the world's policeman."

✪ After the war, the first priority was keeping the peace. One of the decisions made at the meeting of Allied leaders in Yalta (see p. 80) had been to form an international organization devoted to preserving peace. In 1945, the first conference of the United Nations—a term coined by Roosevelt—brought delegates of fifty nations together. Because the war ended with the United States in the strongest position, the headquarters of the U.N. is in New York City.

U.N. Headquarters in New York City.

✪ Popular opinion demanded that those responsible for starting the war be punished. One trial, conducted by eleven nations and held in Tokyo, resulted in the execution in 1948 of numerous Japanese leaders for crimes against humanity and other violations of long-established rules of international law. The Nuremberg Trials of 1945, conducted by the United States, Britain, France, and the Soviet Union, sentenced twenty-two Nazi leaders to death in 1946 for their war crimes. But before the trials, many Nazi officials were able to flee abroad. In 1993, records came to light showing that more than a thousand Nazi war criminals had settled in Argentina, many more than had previously been known. Very few are thought to be still alive.

WAR-CRIMES TRIAL WILL START TODAY

Russian Deputy Prosecutor to Represent Ailing Chief in Nuremberg Court

20 DEFENDANTS TO APPEAR

Kaltenbrunner Is Stricken by Hemorrhage—Krupp's Son to Be Indicted Later

✪ Simon Wiesenthal, a Polish concentration-camp survivor, has devoted the rest of his life to hunting for Nazi criminals and bringing them to justice. One of the nine hundred people he exposed was the Gestapo agent who had seized Anne Frank and her family. Anne's father was the only member of the Secret Annex group to survive the camps. In 1947, he arranged for publication of parts of Anne's diary, fulfilling her dearest wish — to be a published writer. *The Diary of Anne Frank* has sold 20 million copies and is required reading in most American schools. Every year, 600,000 people from all over the world visit the Secret Annex in Amsterdam, in a building now known as the Anne Frank House.

✪ Once Germany had been divided into four zones at Yalta, the Soviet Union isolated its zone as much as possible from those occupied by the Western countries. The Soviet Union had emerged from World War II as the second-most powerful country, and it eventually cut off contact with the rest of the world while it worked to rebuild itself. The barrier it dropped was like an "iron curtain," as Churchill pointed out, preventing travel and the exchange of ideas

German workers build the wall between East and West Berlin.

and goods. In Berlin, the barrier came to be symbolized by a physical wall of concrete and barbed wire, built in 1961 to stem the increasing tide of refugees to Western countries. In 1989, the Berlin Wall was torn down, and East Germany opened its borders to the West.

✪ The end of World War II began the Cold War between the United States and the Soviet Union. It was not a war of fighting, but of paranoia and the development of increasingly more deadly weapons on both sides—weapons with the power to destroy the world. In 1947, the Truman Plan committed the United States to helping other nations resist communist takeover. The United States formed alliances with other non-communist countries and kept one million people in military service; the Soviet Union kept three million. The Cold War lasted over forty years.

⭐ After the damage caused by World War II, cities around the world had to be rebuilt, national economies restored, and millions of refugees relocated. Never in history had so many people been dislocated. Inflation in Germany was so bad that money became worthless; cigarettes were worth

⭐ In 1993, Japan admitted that its Imperial Army had been responsible for the kidnapping, rape, and imprisonment of hundreds of thousands of women from China, Vietnam, Indonesia, the Philippines, and Korea during World War II. Japan formally apologized to the survivors.

Homeless children in London.

⭐ Ironically, Hitler's plan to eliminate Jews resulted instead in the formation of an all-Jewish state. In 1947, the U.N. agreed to divide Palestine into separate Jewish and Arab states, and the independent state of Israel was created on May 14, 1948. Its flag features the Star of David. Among the first Israelis, one out of every three had lost part of their family to the Holocaust. Outside of Israel, the greatest number of Holocaust survivors live in New York City.

more and were used as currency. The United States helped to rebuild Europe with the Marshall Plan, named for Secretary of State George Marshall. Over $13 billion in aid was supplied between 1948 and 1951, in part to prevent the spread of communism.

Jewish children from (left to right) Poland, Latvia, and Hungary on their way to Palestine after release from the Buchenwald concentration camp.

⭐ Under General MacArthur's leadership, 450,000 American troops continued to occupy Japan until 1952. It was a peaceful occupation symbolized by both countries' devotion to baseball (also Japan's national sport). With millions of dollars in aid from the United States, Japan rebuilt itself and gradually became a powerful country again. This time it was as an ally of the United States. Japan was an important trading partner, and was significant in the American fight to stop the spread of communism.

✪ As those who survived the Holocaust grow old and die, the testimony of firsthand witnesses is being lost. Recent polls suggest that some Americans, particularly those with less education, remain ignorant about the Holocaust. There are also people, called "Holocaust deniers," who persist, mostly out of anti-Semitism, in calling the genocide against the Jews a hoax. But more than 4,000 people a day are visiting the United States Holocaust Memorial Museum in Washington, D.C. Many hope that knowledge of the Holocaust can make society more humane. Others are more pessimistic, pointing to present-day "holocausts" around the globe.

✪ There is no Hitler Youth today—under German law, use of Nazi symbols and slogans is forbidden—but traces of age-old racial hatred can be found around the world. In the United States, there are at least 175,000 supporters of hate groups that preach the inferiority of Jews, blacks, Asians, and homosexuals. Some of these groups continue to use Nazi symbolism.

✪ Dwight D. Eisenhower, the war's greatest hero to most Americans, succeeded Truman to become the country's thirty-fourth president in 1952. Familiar with covert operations, he used the CIA to fight the Cold War during his two terms.

✪ After the war, over a hundred top German scientists, led by Wernher von Braun, came here, became citizens, and contributed to our missile and space programs, both peacetime and military. Thus, the development of Hitler's Vengeance weapons led indirectly to man's first landing on the moon. Besides the atomic bomb, other scientific breakthroughs as a result of the war included radar,

sonar, penicillin, DDT, and—as a silicone for use in B-29 bombers—Silly Putty.

✪ Some 15 million Americans lived in a different place than they had before the war. The move of many off the farms turned out to be permanent—one in eight rural Americans never went back. Some began a new lifestyle in rows of identical pastel houses with outdoor barbecues and color-coordinated appliances. Started by William Levitt, Levittowns were suburban developments of houses built for

Levittown, the most notable development in American postwar housing.

returning veterans. Seen by some as dehumanizing, such dwellings came to be a symbol of America's new prosperity. Unable to buy things during the war, people had a lot of money saved up, and their savings kept increasing, from $6 billion in 1945 to $37 billion in 1949. Millions also took advantage of the GI bill of 1944, which offered veterans generous help with education, starting a business, and buying a house. Big businesses got bigger, corner stores became giant supermarkets, and Americans became preoccupied with consumerism and getting ahead.

American astronauts reach the moon in July 1969.

The New York Times

"That's Fit to Print"

VOL CXVIII No 40.721   NEW YORK MONDAY JULY 21 1969   10 CENTS

MEN WALK ON MOON
ASTRONAUTS LAND ON PLAIN;
COLLECT ROCKS, PLANT FLAG

⭐ Almost all working women gave up their jobs when the men came home from war. Traditions had been so ingrained, especially in the media, that everyone went back to them afterward: men defended the country, while women defended the home and family. With few exceptions, gender roles remained stereotyped until the 1960s, when the feminist movement began. The seeds for a major change in American society had been planted—in part because those who had seen their mothers act independently during the war began to question tradition. In 1963, Congress finally passed the Equal Pay Act, guaranteeing equal pay for equal work.

A 1945 advertisement emphasizing gender stereotypes.

Dr. Benjamin Spock, whose first book was published during World War II, changing the way American children are raised.

⭐ Not all wartime marriages lasted: the divorce rate of 1946 broke all records. By 1950, a million veterans had been divorced. Those who divorced were usually quick to remarry, and rates of marriage stayed high.

⭐ Postwar birth rates were so high that a huge new generation was created—the baby boomers, born between 1940 and 1960. By the 1980s, baby boomers were fully one-third of the population of the United States, and their needs and preferences dominated society. The rights of children, who had pulled their own weight during World War II, became more significant afterward. In part due to Dr. Spock, whose *Common Sense Book of Baby and Child Care* sold 40 million copies, child-rearing became more permissive. Before the war, leading guides advised holding babies as little as possible, ignoring their demands. After the war, parents were urged to play with babies and pay attention to their needs.

President John F. Kennedy with Soviet Premier Nikita Khrushchev, Stalin's successor as ruler of the Soviet Union.

✪ In 1960, John F. Kennedy, another World War II hero, became the country's thirty-fifth president. As a twenty-six-year-old Navy lieutenant, he had been much decorated for his heroism as a PT (patrol-torpedo) boat captain in the Pacific.

✪ Most Americans remained staunchly patriotic during the Korean War (1950–53). Hostilities broke out at the 38th parallel between South Korea (controlled by the United States) and North Korea (controlled by the Soviet Union). But during the Vietnam War (1964–75), Americans began to question the government's authority to wage war. The two-fingered "V for Victory" sign from World War II became known as the "peace" sign, symbolizing resistance to the Vietnam War. Many believe that demonstrations against the war hastened its end. There were now two broad groups in America—those who had lived through World War II and those who hadn't. The latter group were not blindly patriotic. And when some became draft resisters who would not go willingly into the military, many World War II veterans disapproved.

Protesters against the Vietnam War in the 1960s.

✪ In 1980, in response to the experiences of Vietnam veterans, the medical establishment officially recognized a disease called posttraumatic stress disorder (PTSD). It covered a range of symptoms that had doubtless affected World War II vets as well—intense fear, numbness, and the constant reliving of traumatic war experiences.

✪ Also in 1980, the former movie star Ronald Reagan became the country's fortieth president. Reagan was one of seven of the last ten United States presidents who played a role in World War II. George Bush, who became the forty-first president in 1988, was a twenty-two-year-old Navy lieutenant forced to bail out of his bombed aircraft during the battle for Okinawa. In 1991, when Bush declared war in the Persian Gulf, he inspired much of the same patriotic unity seen during World War II. Only three recent presidents were not involved in World War II: Jimmy Carter was in the United States Naval Academy at the war's end; Bill Clinton and George W. Bush were born after the war.

Ronald Reagan in a World War II movie called <u>This Is the Army</u>.

✪ In 1948, Truman had finally signed an order guaranteeing equal opportunities for all races in the military. By 1993, blacks, Latinos, and other minorities made up 38 percent of Army forces. The military and civilian career advances made by blacks during World War II proved a direct influence on the legal advances they made during the 1960s civil rights movement.

Colin Powell served as the head of the Joint Chiefs of Staff during the Persian Gulf War and was the highest-ranking leader of the American military. In 2001, President George W. Bush appointed him Secretary of State.

✪ In 1993, the ban against homosexuals in the military was relaxed. Homosexual conduct was prohibited, but homosexuals could not be barred from service just because of their sexual orientation.

✪ American borders opened significantly after World War II. There was widespread agreement that what had happened to the Jews should never be allowed to happen again. In 1951, a United Nations agreement recommended granting asylum to refugees (defined as those persecuted for reasons of race, politics, religion, etc.) who could travel to a safe country on their own. In the United States the Immigration and Naturalization Service administers this program for refugees.

✪ Over time, discrimination against Japanese-Americans eased. But internment had broken the pattern of Japanese immigrants. Instead of living on the West Coast and working on farms, they now live in every state, mostly in cities, and work in virtually all occupations. In 1983, a commission in Congress stated that the detention of Japanese-Americans during World War II was not justified for military necessity, and instead was caused by "race prejudice, war hysteria and a failure of political leadership." Legislation was passed that gave an apology and $20,000 to each Japanese-American affected. But by the time the first payments went out in 1990, more than half of the internees were no longer living.

✪ A notable legacy of World War II is the nostalgia of many Americans who lived though it. To them, those years were our country's finest hour. The end of the war was like the happy ending to a movie: everything was just going to get better and better. Postwar life has gotten increasingly complex and ambiguous, and some wish for a time when life seemed simpler. Whether this wistfulness is based in reality or illusion, it has influenced our personal lives and our national politics.

✪ With the realization that the future of the planet is at stake, there has been worldwide revulsion at the further use of atomic bombs. None have been used to kill people since. Nations have grown much more cautious in championing their superiority over other nations. For over fifty years, the world has continued in an uneasy peace that has survived numerous regional wars without plunging the planet into a World War III.

1919

June 28: Treaty of Versailles signed, finalizing the terms for ending World War I, which included severe retribution against Germany.

1922

Oct. 31: Benito Mussolini becomes Italy's prime minister.

1931

Sept. 18: Japan takes over Manchuria.

1933

Jan. 30: Adolf Hitler becomes German chancellor and begins eliminating opponents.

1934

Aug. 2: Hitler becomes German president.

1935

Sept. 15: Nuremberg Laws deprive Jews of rights of German citizenship.

Oct. 3: Italy invades Ethiopia.

1936

Nov. 25: Germany and Japan sign pact.

1937

July 7: Japan invades China.

1938

Mar. 12: Germany annexes Austria.

Sept. 30: The Munich Pact (signed by Great Britain, France, Italy, and Germany) surrenders Czechoslovakia to Germany.

Nov. 9-10: Crystal Night *(Kristallnacht)* in Germany.

1939

Apr. 7: Italy occupies Albania.

May 22: Italy and Germany sign the Pact of Steel, agreeing to act as a united force.

Sept. 1: Germany invades Poland.

Sept. 1: Evacuation of children from British cities begins.

Sept. 3: Great Britain and France declare war on Germany.

Sept. 5: United States declares its neutrality in European war.

Sept. 9: Canada declares war on Germany.

1940

May 28: Belgium surrenders to Germany, following Denmark, Norway, and the Netherlands.

June 10: Italy declares war on Great Britain and France.

June 11: Australia, New Zealand, and South Africa declare war on Italy.

June 22: France surrenders to Germany.

July 10: Battle of Britain begins.

Sept. 11: Italy attacks Egypt.

Sept. 27: Japan joins the Axis powers of Germany and Italy in the Tripartite Pact.

Oct. 28: Italy invades Greece.

Nov. 6: Franklin D. Roosevelt elected to third term as American president.

Dec. 15: Battle in North Africa begins.

1941

Mar. 11: Lend-Lease Act signed by Roosevelt, providing $7 billion in aid to Britain.

Apr. 6: Germany invades Yugoslavia and Greece.

June 14: United States freezes Axis assets in this country.

June 22: Operation Barbarossa—Germany invades Russia; Italy and Romania declare war on Russia.

July 26: United States suspends all financial and trading relations with Japan.

Oct. 16: Hideki Tojo becomes prime minister of Japan.

Oct. 31: USS *Reuben James* becomes the first American vessel sunk by enemy action.

Dec. 7: Japan attacks Pearl Harbor, Hawaii.

Dec. 7–8: Japanese raids on Guam, Malaya, Manila, Hong Kong, Midway, Wake, Thailand.

Dec. 8: United States declares war on Japan.

Dec. 10: Japan begins invasion of the Philippines.

Dec. 11: Germany and Italy declare war on United States; the United States declares war on them.

1942

Jan. 20: German conference at Wannsee to plan the "Final Solution to the Jewish Problem."

Jan. 26: First U.S. troops arrive in Britain.

Apr. 9: U.S. forces surrender at Bataan.

Apr. 18: First U.S. bombing raid on Tokyo, led by Lieutenant General James Doolittle.

May 22: Mexico declares war on Axis powers.

June 4–7: Battle of Midway, Japan's first major defeat.

June 10: Czech village of Lidice wiped out by Germany.

Nov. 8: United States and Britain invade North Africa.

1943

May 13: Axis troops in North Africa surrender.

Sept. 3: Italy surrenders.

Nov. 18: Battle of Berlin begins.

1944

June 6: D-Day—Allied forces invade Europe at Normandy.

Aug. 25: U.S. and Free French forces enter Paris.

Oct. 20: U.S. forces land at Leyte in the Philippines.

Nov. 7: FDR elected to fourth term as American president.

Dec. 16–30: Battle of the Bulge, which becomes an Allied victory.

1945

Feb 4–11: Yalta Conference in Russia, at which Roosevelt, Churchill, and Stalin meet to plan postwar Europe.

Feb. 19: U. S. Marines land on Iwo Jima.

Apr. 1: U.S. Marines land on Okinawa.

Apr. 12: FDR dies and Vice-President Harry S Truman becomes president.

Apr. 16: Beginning of Russian offensive against Berlin.

Apr. 28: Mussolini is executed.

Apr. 30: Hitler commits suicide.

May 2: German forces in Italy surrender.

May 8: V-E Day—Germany surrenders unconditionally to Allied forces.

June 26: Charter of United Nations signed by fifty countries at San Francisco Conference.

July 4: Occupation of Berlin by four countries takes effect.

July 16: First atomic bomb exploded at Alamogordo, New Mexico.

Aug. 6: Atomic bomb dropped on Hiroshima, Japan.

Aug. 9: Atomic bomb dropped on Nagasaki, Japan.

Aug. 14: V-J Day—Japan surrenders.

Nov. 20: First German war-crimes trial begins in Nuremberg.

1946

Apr. 10: Japanese war-crimes trial begins in Tokyo.

Oct. 16: Execution of principal German war criminals.

1947

June 5: Marshall Plan for European recovery proposed.

1948

May 14: Creation of Israel.

Dec. 23: Execution of principal Japanese war criminals.

BIBLIOGRAPHY

"What you're making may save my Daddy's life"

World War II is a never-ending subject for study, with new books published every year on various aspects of it. Here are those that were used in the creation of this book. (Books especially for young readers are marked with an asterisk.)

WORLD WAR II—GENERAL

*Hoobler, Dorothy and Thomas. *An Album of World War II.* New York: Franklin Watts, 1977.

Koppes, Clayton. *Hollywood Goes to War.* New York: Free Press, 1987.

Life magazine. *Life Goes to War: A Picture History of World War II.* Boston: Little, Brown, 1977.

O'Neill, William L. *A Democracy at War: America's Fight at Home and Abroad in World War II.* New York: Free Press, 1993.

Roeder, George. *The Censored War: American Visual Experience During World War II.* New Haven: Yale University Press, 1993.

*Sullivan, George. *The Day Pearl Harbor Was Bombed: A Photo History of World War II.* New York: Scholastic, 1991.

Terkel, Studs. *"The Good War": An Oral History of World War Two.* New York: Pantheon Books, 1984.

Time-Life Books. *World War II*. 39 volumes. Alexandria, Virginia: Time-Life
Books, 1976–85.

*The World at Arms: The Reader's Digest Illustrated History of World War
II*. London: Reader's Digest Association, 1989.

THE HOME FRONT

Cohen, Stan. *V for Victory: America's Home Front During World War II*.
Missoula, Montana: Pictorial Histories Publishing, 1991.

*Lawson, Don. *An Album of World War II Home Fronts*. New York:
Franklin Watts, 1980.

Tuttle, William M. *"Daddy's Gone to War": The Second World War in the
Lives of America's Children*. New York: Oxford University Press, 1993.

*Whitman, Sylvia. *V Is for Victory: The American Home Front During
World War II*. Minneapolis: Lerner, 1993.

IN UNIFORM

*Bliven, Bruce, Jr. *The Story of D-Day: June 6, 1944*. New York: Random
House, 1984.

*Whitman, Sylvia. *Uncle Sam Wants You: Military Men and Women of
World War II*. Minneapolis: Lerner, 1993.

*Windrow, Martin. *The World War II GI*. New York: Franklin Watts, 1986.

WOMEN AND MINORITIES

Bernstein, Alison. *American Indians and World War II: Toward a New Era in Indian Affairs.* Norman: University of Oklahoma Press, 1991.

*Colman, Penny. *Rosie the Riveter: Women Working on the Home Front in World War II.* New York: Alfred A. Knopf Books for Young Readers, 1995.

Gluck, Sherna Berger. *Rosie the Riveter Revisited: Women, the War, and Social Change.* Boston: Twayne, 1987.

Potter, Lou, with William Miles and Nina Rosenblum. *Liberators: Fighting on Two Fronts in World War II.* New York: Harcourt Brace Jovanovich, 1992.

Weatherford, Doris. *American Women and World War II.* New York: Facts on File, 1990.

JAPANESE-AMERICAN INTERNMENT CAMPS

*Brimner, Larry Dane. *Voices from the Camps: Internment of Japanese Americans During World War II.* New York: Franklin Watts, 1994.

*Davis, Daniel. *Behind Barbed Wire: The Imprisonment of Japanese Americans During World War II.* New York: Dutton, 1982.

*Houston, Jeanne Wakatsuki and James. *Farewell to Manzanar.* Boston: Houghton Mifflin, 1973.

*Stanley, Jerry. *I Am an American: A True Story of Japanese Internment.* New York: Crown Publishers, 1994.

NAZI GERMANY AND THE HOLOCAUST

*Frank, Anne. *The Diary of Anne Frank: The Critical Edition.* New York: Doubleday, 1989.

*Friedman, Ina. *The Other Victims: First-Person Stories of Non-Jews Persecuted by the Nazis.* Boston: Houghton Mifflin, 1990.

*Heyes, Eileen. *Children of the Swastika: The Hitler Youth.* Brookfield, Conn.: Millbrook Press, 1993.

*Opdyke, Irene Gut, with Jennifer Armstrong. *In My Hands: Memories of a Holocaust Rescuer.* New York: Knopf, 1999.

Keneally, Thomas. *Schindler's List*. New York: Simon & Schuster, 1982.

Lipstadt, Deborah. *Denying the Holocaust: The Growing Assault on Truth and Memory*. New York: Free Press, 1993.

*Lowry, Lois. *Number the Stars*. Boston: Houghton Mifflin, 1989.

*Meltzer, Milton. *Never to Forget: The Jews of the Holocaust*. New York: Harper & Row, 1976.

*—. *Rescue: The Story of How Gentiles Saved Jews in the Holocaust*. New York: Harper & Row, 1988.

*Rogasky, Barbara. *Smoke and Ashes: The Story of the Holocaust*. New York: Holiday House, 1988.

Shirer, William. *The Rise and Fall of the Third Reich: A History of Nazi Germany*. New York: Simon & Schuster, 1960.

Time-Life Books. *The Third Reich.* 18 volumes. Alexandria, Virginia: Time-Life Books, 1988–1991.

*Van der Rol, Ruud, and Rian Verhoeven. *Anne Frank: Beyond the Diary*. New York: Viking, 1993.

CODES AND SPIES

*Aaseng, Nathan. *Navajo Code Talkers*. New York: Walker, 1992.

*Lawson, Don. *The Secret World War II*. New York: Franklin Watts, 1978.

*Silverstein, Herma. *Spies Among Us: The Truth About Modern Espionage*. New York: Franklin Watts, 1988.

*Sweeney, James. *True Spy Stories*. New York: Franklin Watts, 1981.

THE ATOM BOMB

*Black, Wallace. *Hiroshima and the Atomic Bomb.* New York: Crestwood House, 1993.

Hersey, John. *Hiroshima.* New York: Knopf, 1946.

Rhodes, Richard. *The Making of the Atomic Bomb.* New York: Simon & Schuster, 1986.

PERSONALITIES

*Cannon, Marian. *Dwight David Eisenhower: War Hero and President.* New York: Franklin Watts, 1990.

Fest, Joachim. *The Face of the Third Reich: Portraits of the Nazi Leadership.* New York: Pantheon Books, 1970.

Flood, Charles. *Hitler: The Path to Power.* Boston: Houghton Mifflin, 1989.

*Freedman, Russell. *Franklin Delano Roosevelt.* New York: Clarion, 1990.

*__. *Eleanor Roosevelt: A Life of Discovery.* New York: Clarion, 1993.

Gilbert, Martin. *Churchill: A Photographic Portrait.* Boston: Houghton Mifflin, 1988.

Gun, Nerin. *Eva Braun: Hitler's Mistress.* New York: Meredith Press, 1968.

*Hoobler, Dorothy and Thomas. *Showa: The Age of Hirohito.* New York: Walker, 1990.

Hoyt, Edwin. *Warlord: Tojo Against the World.* Lanham, Maryland: Scarborough House, 1993.

*Lyttle, Richard. *Il Duce: The Rise and Fall of Benito Mussolini.* New York: Atheneum, 1987.

Manchester, William. *American Caesar: Douglas MacArthur, 1880–1964.* Boston: Little, Brown, 1978.

*Marrin, Albert. *Hitler.* New York: Viking, 1987.

*—. *Stalin: Russia's Man of Steel.* New York: Viking, 1988.

McCullough, David. *Truman.* New York: Simon & Schuster, 1992.

*Rummel, Jack. *Robert Oppenheimer: Dark Prince.* New York: Facts on File, 1992.

*Whitelaw, Nancy. *A Biography of General Charles de Gaulle.* New York: Dillon, 1991.

PICTURE CREDITS

All photographs are from the National Archives, with the following exceptions:

Jacket front: UPI/Bettman.

Chapter 1. Page 6—*girl in Poland*: © Julien Bryan/International Film Foundation. Page 7— *British soldier*: © Hulton Deutsch. Page 8—*Depression-era family*: AP/Wide World Photos.

Chapter 2. Page 12—*California newsboy*: courtesy of the Library of Congress. Page 14—*servicemen*: courtesy of the Library of Congress. Page 14—*recruiting poster*: courtesy of the Library of Congress. Pages 14-15—*rally*: courtesy of the Library of Congress.

Chapter 3. Page 25—*nursery school*: courtesy of the Library of Congress. Pages-27— *crowds*: courtesy of the Library of Congress. Page 28-29—*Marine's family*: courtesy of the Library of Congress. Page 29—*Superman*: courtesy of the Library of Congress.

Chapter 4. Page 31—*draftee*: George Strock/*Life* magazine, © Time Warner. Page 40—*the Andrews Sisters*: courtesy of the Library of Congress.

Chapter 5. Page 46—*Hitler Youth*: © Hulton Deutsch. Page 47—*broken windows*: courtesy of the United States Holocaust Memorial Museum. Page 48—*Polish Jews*: © UPI/Bettman. Page 50—*Anne Frank*: © AFF/Anne Frank House, Amsterdam. Page 51—*Oskar Schindler*: courtesy the United States Holocaust Memorial Museum.

Chapter 6. Page 54—*car being searched*: courtesy of the Library of Congress. Pages 54—*Little Tokyo*: courtesy of the Library of Congress. Page 55—*cattle trucks*: courtesy of the Library of Congress. Page 55—*train*: courtesy of the Library of Congress. Pages 56-57—*boy with hat*: courtesy of the Library of Congress. Page 57—*new housing*: courtesy of the Library of Congress. Page 58 *Christmas*: courtesy of the Library of Congress..

Chapter 7. Page 60—*FDR*: AP/Wide World Photos. Page 63—*Adolf Hitler with boy*: Heinrich Hoffman/Bayerische Staatsbibliothek Munchen.

Chapter 8. Page 75—*book with gun*: Erich Lessing/Art Resource. Page 76—*The Best Years of Our Lives*: courtesy of the Library of Congress. Page 77—*Casablanca*: Culver Pictures, Inc.

Chapter 9. Page 79—*newspaper headline*: © 1944 by the New York Times Company.

Chapter 10. Page 91—*United Nations*: The Image Bank. Page 92—*newspaper headline*: © 1945 by the New York Times Company. Pages 94—*newspaper headline*: © 1969 by the New York Times Company. Page 94-95—*Levittown*: courtesy of the Library of Congress. Pages 95—*Dr. Benjamin Spock*: courtesy of the Library of Congress. Page 96-97—*war protesters*: © UPI/Bettman. Page 97—*This Is the Army*: courtesy of the Library of Congress. Page 97—*Colin Powell*: courtesy of the Library of Congress.

All photographs reprinted by permission.